101
Gift Projects
from Wood

◇

◇

James A. Jacobson

Sterling Publishing Co., Inc.   New York

Dedication

For some gifts I've received . . .

Anita
Karen and Mike
Peter and Kathy
Ann and Chris
Christin, Jessica and
Mallory

Library of Congress Cataloging-in-Publication Data

Jacobson, James A.
   101 gift projects from wood / James A. Jacobson.
      p.   cm.
   Includes index.
   ISBN 0-8069-8418-X
   1. Woodwork.   I. Title.   II. Title: One hundred one gift
projects from wood.
TT180.J26   1992
674'.8–dc20   91-41320
                                                   CIP

10   9   8   7   6   5   4   3   2

Published in 1992 by Sterling Publishing Company, Inc.
387 Park Avenue South, New York, N.Y. 10016
© 1992 by James A. Jacobson
Distributed in Canada by Sterling Publishing
% Canadian Manda Group, P.O. Box 920, Station U
Toronto, Ontario, Canada M8Z 5P9
Distributed in Great Britain and Europe by Cassell PLC
Villiers House, 41/47 Strand, London WC2N 5JE, England
Distributed in Australia by Capricorn Link Ltd.
P.O. Box 665, Lane Cove, NSW 2066
Manufactured in the United States of America
All rights reserved

Sterling ISBN 0-8069-8418-X

Contents

INTRODUCTION

Gift-giving is a major activity in the lives of most of us. Note the gift-based days that most of us acknowledge. In addition to Christmas, Valentine's Day, Mothers Day, Fathers Day, and Grandparents Day, we have birthdays, anniversaries, confirmations, weddings, baby showers, and graduations. This list does not, of course, include those more personal occasions that some of us recognize with a gift as, for example, the promotion of a friend at work or a housewarming party. The occasions where we feel the need to give a gift seem endless.

It may be time to consider making some of your gifts. There are many good reasons to consider this possibility. First, think of the money you could save. A handmade gift will cost considerably less than a store-bought gift.

An equally important reason for making your own gifts is that people, as a rule, enjoy receiving gifts that have been made specifically for them, especially when made by the gift-giver. It conveys a sense of caring and importance that is not communicated by some item from a gift shop.

Making gifts is also an enjoyable way of using leisure time. For those who do not have much leisure time, gift-making could even prove therapeutic. The experiences of working with your hands, meeting the challenges presented by a particular project, and having something of value at the end of your labors are positive ones.

Gift-making also gives those unfamiliar with woodworking exposure to it with a minimal investment. As you will discover, any number of the gift projects can be made with hand tools or some inexpensive electric tools, all of which you will learn to use. When making the projects, you will shop for and learn about the different kinds of woods that are available.

If you become relatively adept at making gifts

and want to supplement your income, craft shows may be for you. Most people doing craft shows seem to have started their business as a result of a hobby. Craft shows can prove productive.

The various gift projects presented in this book can be crafted as presented or modified as desired. Some individuals enjoy making the projects as shown, following the step-by-step directions. Others are more inclined to modify a project, that is, to change its design or size to meet a particular requirement or taste.

The same approach, as you will note, can be used when adding a finish to a project. While I may indicate that a project should be painted or stained, your preference may be for a clear lacquer finish.

You will also note that the various designing and crafting procedures are enumerated for each project. While the primary intent is to assist you in making a gift, a secondary hope is that you will learn techniques to design and craft your own projects. While it is great fun to make the various gift projects, it is also quite satisfying to learn the proper way to make them.

The projects in this book range from simple to complex, and will challenge both beginning and experienced woodworkers. Some readers, however, may be unable to make a particular project because they lack the tool needed. An example of this would be some of the wood-turning projects, which require a lathe. In many instances, you may be able to use the tool in a high school's or community college's woodwork shop. On the other hand, it may be time for you to buy the tool or tools you've always wanted and become more involved in woodworking. Making the gift projects in this book with your new tools would be a great way to begin.

James A. Jacobson

TOOLS AND ACCESSORIES

With a few exceptions, most of the gift projects presented in the following pages can be crafted with small power tools and some hand tools. For those who have several of the larger floor-model power tools, the projects can be made more quickly and, if desired, in quantity.

If you're new to woodworking, you may want to consider purchasing or using the small power tools. These are readily available from a variety of sources, including local hardware stores, discount outlets, and mail-order stores. Additionally, the use of the smaller power tools significantly reduces your investment.

You may, as you get more involved in woodworking, also want to purchase some of the larger floor-model tools. With the exception of a wood lathe, you do not need them for the gift projects presented. If you do not have a floor-model tool and would like to use one, inquire at the woodworking shop in your local high school or community college. These are excellent resources for the beginning woodworker, especially when you want to minimize your investment.

In addition to the various tools, a variety of tool accessories are needed. These include bits for electric drills and routers, and a variety of abrasive grits for power sanders. Some tools you may want to use need burrs and other accessories for removing wood more quickly when carving. In many instances, you can improvise to minimize your costs. Specific accessories needed for a particular gift project are described in the project directions.

If you need to buy tools and accessories, shop around. The tool market is very competitive, and you have lots of tools to choose from. As a rule, it pays to buy quality tools. Purchase several issues of the various national woodworking magazines that are on the market. In addition to good

information on woodworking, you will find listings and ads from the various mail-order tool suppliers. Request catalogues and other information from these suppliers, so that you can become an informed consumer.

Shop also at your local hardware stores and discount houses. Talk to people you know who have some woodworking tools. Go to a craft show and talk to woodworkers. Visit the local high school or college and talk to the shop teachers.

Good sources of non-powered hand tools are flea markets, yard sales, and auctions. While it's always fun to buy a new tool, excellent used tools can be bought at these events. In many instances, the tools have been cleaned and refurbished.

Get a sense of what new hand tools cost in the local stores before buying at these various events. This will help you in making better decisions when you're shopping for used tools. Incidentally, some of these older tools are of better quality than new tools.

In that woodworking is a series of related tasks, a good way to introduce you to tools and their accessories is to explore these specific tasks. While there are some exceptions, this approach is generally helpful in showing how the various tasks and tools are related. As you will discover, the various accessories allow the tools to do a wider range of tasks, and some very specific tasks.

Before moving on to the specific tasks, pay attention to the following words of advice concerning power tools: No matter what power tool you use, become familiar with its operation by thoroughly studying the manual or taking a class. Always wear safety glasses or a face shield of some kind (Illus. 1). Wear the appropriate clothing and use safety devices.

Measuring

The most common mistakes made when crafting a gift are measuring mistakes. Either the board is measured too long or short, or some other kind of measuring error is made.

Some of the measuring tasks in woodworking are so obvious that it is easy to be careless and make mistakes. While measuring is not one of the more exciting woodworking tasks, it certainly is one of the most critical.

Many woodworkers, to avoid mistakes when measuring for a project, use the metric system. With few exceptions, most measuring devices are available with metric dimensions. This eliminates the need to measure in fractions of an inch, which is a problem for many woodworkers. You may want to consider buying and using measuring devices employing the metric system or that have both the imperial and metric system imprinted on them.

A metal tape measure will prove useful when you purchase lumber or are making a project. There are many different types available. The type you will buy is determined by how much money you are willing to spend.

A 12-foot-long tape is usually adequate for most measuring tasks. Seldom will you buy lumber for woodworking that is longer than 12 feet unless you have a truck to haul it home. Measuring tapes are available in various widths, including widths of ½, ¾, and 1 inch. The wider tapes are easier to read.

Standard metal rulers will also be helpful in measuring tasks, when cutting glass, or if you need a straight edge when cutting something with a utility knife or razor blade. I have a 12-inch rubber-back steel ruler and a 36-inch steel ruler in my shop. They're indispensable, and they don't break like their wooden counterparts.

For making straight cutting lines, especially if you're using a hand saw, consider buying a try square (Illus. 2). When this square is used, the handle slips over the edge of a board and the blade lays flat on the surface. Run a pencil along the edge of the blade and mark the cutting line on the board. It's an invaluable device when you want square cuts on a board. A try square can be found at a flea market or similar place at a reasonable price.

Illus. 2. Try square (photo courtesy of Stanley® Tools).

Graduations are marked on the blade of a try square, so the tool can also be used for a variety of measuring tasks. While not a mandatory tool for making gift projects, it will prove helpful if you're cutting your boards with a hand saw or hand sabre saw. It's hard to make a straight cut if you don't have a square line to follow.

An alternative to a try square is a combination square (Illus. 3). This square is more versatile. Another option to consider is a large steel square. Any one of these devices will serve you well in crafting the various projects.

Another useful and inexpensive measuring device is a school compass. It will prove valuable when you are making round mirrors or round cutting boards. In addition to its point-and-pencil circle-making capability, it has a graduated scale for making the circles the size needed.

There are many other interesting devices for measuring that are on the market. Browse the tool catalogues and the local hardware and dis-

Illus. 3. *Combination square (photo courtesy of Stanley Tools).*

Illus. 4. *Torpedo level (photo courtesy of Stanley Tools).*

count stores. One other item you may want to purchase is a small torpedo level (Illus. 4). While not a measuring device per se, it's indispensable when you are hanging a shelf.

Sawing

While a handsaw (Illus. 5) and a coping saw (Illus. 6) can be used to do project sawing tasks,

Illus. 5. *Handsaw (photo courtesy of Stanley Tools).*

Illus. 6. *Coping saw (photo courtesy of Stanley Tools).*

you will find a power tool to be more useful. As with most woodworking, the activity you will do the most when making these projects is sawing. It is recommended that you have at least one hand power tool or, if you can afford it, a floor-model power tool. Some of these tools are examined below.

A sabre saw (Illus. 7) is a versatile saw. This hand-held tool will not only make straight cuts, but also decorative cuts. With a few exceptions, most of your project-sawing can be made with this type of tool. There are also a variety of saw blades available for sabre saws (Illus. 8). As a rule, a blade that will make fine or scroll cuts will prove the most useful. If you have a circular saw (Illus. 9), use it for making straight cuts, and the sabre saw for decorative cuts. Carefully read the tool manual before operating the tool. The manual will not only help you to learn how to use the tool safely, but also how to more effectively saw with it.

Illus. 7. Sabre saw (photo courtesy of Porter Cable Power Tools).

Illus. 8. Sabre-saw blades (photo courtesy of Stanley Tools).

Illus. 9. Circular saw (photo courtesy of Porter Cable Power Tools).

For those who favor floor power tools to accomplish their sawing tasks, consider a table saw (Illus. 10) or a radial arm saw (Illus. 11). Either tool will do a wide variety of sawing tasks. Before using a floor power tool, make sure that you read the manual and are totally familiar with the tool. Carefully follow each and every safety rule in the manual when using these tools.

A table saw and radial arm saw are considerably more expensive than the hand power tools. If you are considering woodworking as a hobby or want to make gift projects in quantity, then they may be a worthwhile investment.

Another saw that may prove helpful is a band saw (Illus. 12). In addition to making some

Illus. 10. Table saw (photo courtesy of Delta International Machinery Corp.).

Illus. 11. Radial arm saw (photo courtesy of Delta International Machinery Corp.).

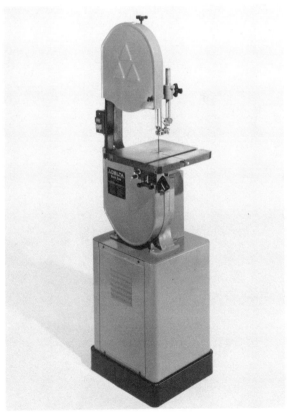

Illus. 12. Band saw (photo courtesy of Delta International Machinery Corp.).

straight cuts, it can also make decorative cuts if a small saw blade is used. Many of the gift projects can be quickly made with a band saw.

There are many different types and sizes of band saws available, including a bench or table-top saw (Illus. 13). Blades are an important part of the successful use of this tool. As with most of the large tools, in addition to the manual, there are a number of books on the market that will prove instructive.

While you may want to use a mitre box and saw (Illus. 14), the easiest and most accurate tool for making mitres is an electric mitre saw (Illus. 15). Several projects employ frames that have mitre cuts. While an electric mitre saw is ideal for sawing mitres, you can also make them with a

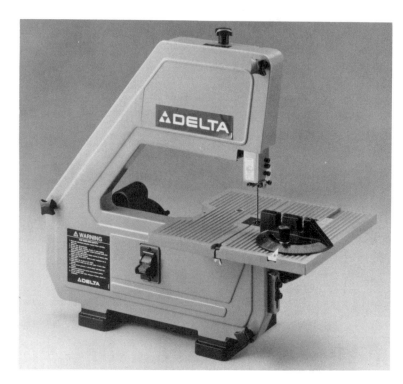

Illus. 13. Tabletop band saw (photo courtesy of Delta International Machinery Corp.).

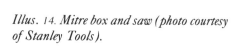

Illus. 14. Mitre box and saw (photo courtesy of Stanley Tools).

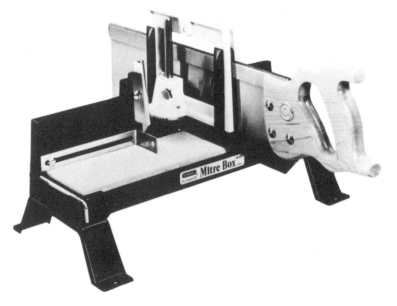

Illus. 15. Electric mitre saw (photo courtesy of Delta International Machinery Corp.).

Illus. 16. Variable-speed scroll saw (photo courtesy of Delta International Machinery Corp.).

sabre saw, a table saw, or a radial arm saw. The accuracy of the cut is more important than the tool that makes the cut. Mitre joints have to fit tightly together. If you should buy a power mitre saw, read the tool directions and precautions carefully. A power mitre saw, as any other power saw, can be an unforgiving tool.

In recent years, the floor-model scroll saw has become one of the most popular tools on the market (Illus. 16). For intricate and detailed sawing, this type of tool is the best. It is capable of cutting a variety of materials of diverse thicknesses. With the appropriate saw blade, the tool can make almost any decorative cut.

While many of the gift projects can be sawed using this tool, the sabre saw also does a respectable job for considerably less money. If you are considering woodworking as a hobby, you may want to consider a scroll saw. It is a very productive tool and is fun to use. There are also many different types of scroll saws on the market, including a bench or tabletop saw (Illus. 17).

Drilling

Many of the projects require that you have the capacity to drill holes. Some woodworkers may be inclined to using a standard brace and bit. For those who enjoy working wood with traditional non-power hand tools, the brace and bit are a joy to use. Unfortunately, they do not have the ca-

Illus. 17. *Bench scroll saw (photo courtesy of Delta International Machinery Corp.).*

pability to do many of the drilling tasks that the projects require. An electric hand drill (Illus. 18) will be much more useful. The electric drill will provide the kind of power needed for many of the projects. It will also accommodate a variety of drill accessories that you will find helpful when crafting the projects.

Illus. 18. *Electric drill (photo courtesy of Makita U.S.A. Tools).*

In that there are many different kinds of electric hand drills on the market, shop at both the local stores and the mail-order suppliers. You may already have one around, as hand electric drills are found in most households. If you have to buy a drill, spend slightly more money for a quality tool that has at least a ⅜-inch chuck and adequate power. Adequate power and a larger chuck become very important when you use some drill accessories or make a project from one of the hardwoods.

Two other features should be considered if you plan to buy a power hand drill. One is variable speed. This feature literally allows you to vary the speed at which the tool operates. This is important when you are using some accessories.

Another feature to consider when buying a drill is its capacity to reverse its rotation. A drill with reversible rotation will run in the opposite direction if you push a switch. This is a useful feature if you need to remove a stuck bit or screw. Neither of these features add much to the cost of the tool.

If you're already a serious woodworker and

need a tool for drilling, consider a floor-model drill press (Illus. 19). There are also bench-model drill presses available that have many of the same features. A floor-model drill press enables you to do more accurate drilling, and has more power. It also has a larger chuck, which enables you to use more accessories.

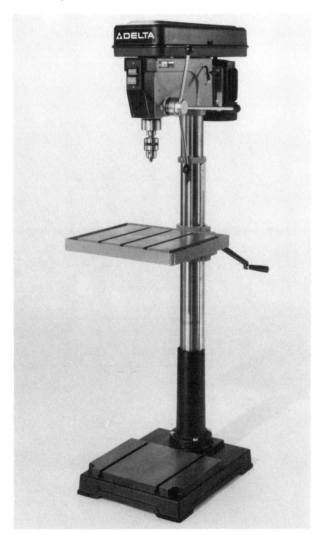

Illus. 19. Drill press (photo courtesy of Delta International Machinery Corp.).

In order for any of these drills to be useful, they must have a bit in place. It is the bit that does the actual drilling of the hole. While some bits are designed to drill metal, others are used exclusively in wood. You will find, however, that many of the high-speed-steel twist bits, designed for use in metal, can also be used in wood (Illus.

20). These types of bits come in a wide variety of sizes and are relatively inexpensive.

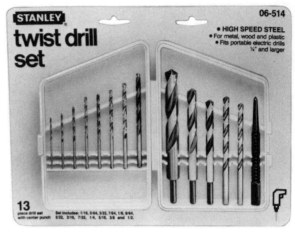

Illus. 20. Twist drill set (photo courtesy of Stanley Tools).

There are a number of bits that are designed specifically for use in wood. One of these bits is called the spade bit (Illus. 21). The spade bit comes in several diameters, and can be effectively used in both an electric hand drill or a drill press. Spade bits are readily available in stores selling tools or by mail-order catalogues.

One bit that is more effective than the spade bit, and also more expensive, is the power-bore bit (Illus. 22). This type of bit tends to drill into

Illus. 21. Spade bits (photo courtesy of Stanley Tools).

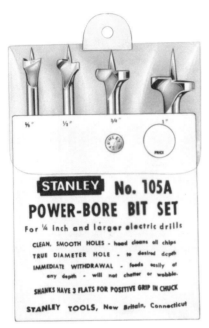

Illus. 22. Power-bore bits (photo courtesy of Stanley Tools).

woodworking. The multi-spur and larger Forstner bit can only be used in a drill press. As you become more involved in woodworking, you will want to consider purchasing these kinds of bits.

In addition to the above drilling accessories, you will find an array of other devices on the market. One that you may find useful when crafting projects is a plug cutter. Rather than cutting plugs from dowels or buying commercial ones, you can use a plug cutter to make your own.

Illus. 23. Screw-sinks (photo courtesy of Stanley Tools).

wood with less effort, and more accurately. A power-bore bit is good to use when you have to drill holes accurately. Power-bore bits are also effective when screws and plugs are used to assemble a project.

In several of the projects in this book, wood screws are used to assemble various components. You may also decide to use screws on some of the other projects. As a rule, when using screws drill a pilot hole and a counter-sink area to accommodate the screw head. Always drill the pilot hole so that it's smaller than the screw diameter, to prevent the wood from cracking. For these kinds of tasks, consider using screw-sinks (Illus. 23). Another option is to use a high-speed twist bit and a standard countersink (Illus. 24).

For drilling larger holes for projects, consider using a hole saw (Illus. 25). This type of accessory is available in various diameters, and can be used with a hand power drill as well as a drill press. Another device, to be used only on a drill press, is a circle cutter (Illus. 26). This is a functional cutter that can make holes ranging from 1⅛ to 8 ¼ inches in diameter. This device is used on a number of projects.

Other bits designed for wood that may prove helpful are Forstner bits and multi-spur bits. While expensive, these bits are excellent for

Illus. 24. Countersink (photo courtesy of Stanley Tools).

14

Illus. 25. *Hole saw (photo courtesy of Stanley Tools).*

Illus. 27. *Router (photo courtesy of Porter Cable Power Tools).*

While the router can be effectively used by holding it in your hands, a router table gives it more versatility (Illus. 28). The table, with the router mounted underneath, allows more control of the routing process and more uses for the tool. Consider buying a router table.

The router is a very noisy and intimidating tool. It has a sharp, steel bit that revolves at about 25,000 revolutions per minute. Read the manual

Illus. 26. *Circle cutter (photo courtesy of Stanley Tools).*

Routing

Many of the projects require the use of a router (Illus. 27) or some other tool that will shape or make specific cuts in wood.

The router is the most used and versatile tool in the woodworking shop. If you don't have one, consider purchasing one. You will find that like the saw and drill, the router is mandatory for woodworking.

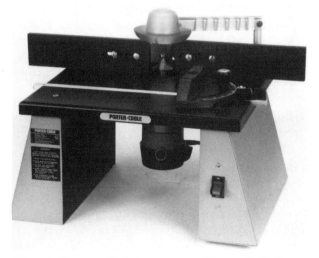

Illus. 28. *Router table (photo courtesy of Porter Cable Power Tools).*

that comes with the tool and follow all safety procedures.

To accomplish the various routing tasks, high-speed-steel or carbide bits are secured in the router (Illus. 29). There are many different bits available that shape the edges of a project or board. Some bits round over the edges, while others make a cove or ogee cut. Other bits will cut out an area on a mirror frame that allows you to inset a piece of mirror. Some straight bits are used to cut grooves into the surface of boards which, in turn, hold shelves in place. You will find that there is a router bit for most wood shaping tasks.

Illus. 29. Router bits (photo courtesy of Stanley Tools).

When projects require the use of a router, specifics regarding its setup and the type of bit needed are given. You will develop some expertise in using the router after doing several gift projects.

In that most hardware and discount stores stock routers, router tables, and a variety of bits, shop around. Review current issues of the various national woodworking magazines for sales from mail-order suppliers. Some companies sell only router bits at very competitive prices. Buy a tool that has sufficient power to do the kinds of jobs that will be required of it. In most instances, a 1 horsepower router is adequate. There are some excellent books on routers that you may want to read prior to purchasing the tool.

Turning

There are several projects that require the use of a wood lathe (Illus. 30). Wood turning is a truly enjoyable activity. While many woodworkers have a lathe to turn the various gift projects, others may have to consider using one at the local school. In that a lathe is rather expensive and also requires an array of turning tools and other supplies, wood turning represents a major financial undertaking. Seek out an opportunity to try wood turning before making the investment. There are also some excellent books on wood turning that you should examine.

Most of the gift projects that involve wood turning can be done by either the beginning or experienced woodturner, using either a cut piece, some scrap, or a combination of the two. Opportunities to do both faceplate- and spindle-turning can be found in the various projects. Thus, they represent a good introduction to one area of woodworking that you might want to pursue as a hobby.

Carving

Carving is an activity that can quickly become habit forming. In addition to being very relaxing, it can be done with a minimum of space and tools. There are many different techniques, tools, and accessories involved in carving. Some woodworkers, in fact, also consider whittling, in which you only need a piece of wood and a jackknife. You may prefer to use a combination of hand and power tools, along with types of wood that lend themselves to carving.

As you will find out when making the projects, most pieces that will be carved have to first be rough-cut to shape with a band saw. A tool that will serve you well in further shaping your project is an electric grinder (Illus. 31). Using large carbide burrs, the grinder allows you to remove lots of wood quickly while shaping the project. Also consider using a sloyd or carving knife. These are all potentially dangerous tools, and need to be used carefully.

Illus. 30. Wood lathe (photo courtesy of Delta International Machinery Corp.).

Illus. 31. Electric grinder (photo courtesy of Makita U.S.A., Inc.).

Another tool that you may find useful in carving gift projects and other projects is a rotary tool (Illus. 32). When used with various accessories, a rotary tool can also remove wood, shape a project, and add detail to a carving. A related tool that is also effective employs a flexible shaft, motor, and handpiece. These small electric tools, given the variety of accessories available, can be very helpful in power-carving the projects.

Details can also be created on carvings with a wide variety of carving tools or a carving knife. There are a variety of palm-handled carving sets on the market that can be useful. These sets give the beginner a sampling of the most commonly used carving tools at an affordable price. Several mail-order catalogues have a full line of carving tools and accessories. Check the national wood-

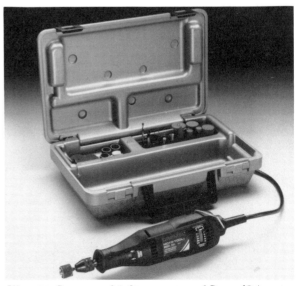

Illus. 32. Rotary tool (photo courtesy of Dremel®).

working magazines for many of these sources. There are also in some larger communities specialty shops that cater to the woodworker and stock an array of carving supplies. Finally, there are excellent books on the market that will assist you in furthering your interest in carving.

Another tool that is necessary for most of the projects but is also very helpful when carving is an electric finishing sander (Illus. 33). Used with coarse-grit abrasives, the small sanders can remove wood and shape the project as desired. In some instances, the sander is the tool to use when carving a project. Many of the small sanders are equipped with a dust bag, which contains the dust when these tools are used. If you purchase a finishing sander, consider one with a dust-collecting capability.

Illus. 33. Finishing sander (photo courtesy of Makita U.S.A., Inc.).

There are many rasps and files that are very useful in shaping the carved projects (Illus. 34). Look for rasps that have a rough surface. Files are usually used on metal, and lack the rough surface of the rasp. Flea markets and auctions can be good sources of rasps and files at reasonable prices.

In many communities there are wood-carving clubs that you may find of interest. Most are for beginning carvers. They can be an excellent way to learn how to carve properly. In many instances, they can be helpful in providing information on where to purchase carving tools, what

kinds to buy, and how best to use them. Many of these clubs also have periodic shows that are open to the public.

Illus. 34. Rasp and file (photo courtesy of Stanley Tools).

Sanding and Surface Preparation

All projects need to be sanded or have their surfaces properly prepared prior to finishing. While an effective way to prepare surfaces is to use abrasive paper with various grits and a block of wood, a finishing sander (Illus. 33) is easier and more effective. Power greatly simplifies the job, and will also yield better results. The small finishing sanders can be easily held in one hand and applied to almost all project surfaces and edges. As indicated earlier, there are many different brands on the market, so shop around.

A belt sander (Illus. 35) has more power than a finishing sander, and can be used for a wider range of jobs. The size of a belt sander is determined by the sanding belt. Some belt sanders have an optional disc sander capability. In addition to surface-sanding, these tools can also be used for limited shaping work when you are carving. With a coarse-grit belt, a belt sander can remove a lot of wood quickly when you are shaping a carving project. This is the kind of sander you will want if you're considering doing serious woodworking as a hobbyist. As with any of the power tools, determine the type of sander you want and then shop around.

If you do not have a router to round edges on the projects, consider using a small block plane (Illus. 36). When properly set, they are excellent for removing sharp edges. Abrasive paper will complete the task. A plane is a seldom-used tool that is great to have when needed; this is especially true of the small block planes.

Illus. 35. Belt sander (photo courtesy of Delta International Machinery Corp.).

Illus. 36. Block plane (photo courtesy of Stanley Tools).

the local lumberyard and the metal brackets. If a piece of plywood is secured to the sawhorses, they can also serve as a functional workbench.

Some useful cutting tools that are worth having are a utility knife (Illus. 39) and a hobby knife (Illus. 40). Both have replaceable blades and have many uses around the shop. The hobby knife can be used for detailed work when you are carving. The utility knife can be used for all kinds of cutting tasks.

Each project contains specifics on surface preparation, the types of abrasive grits to use, and the sanding technique. You need to anticipate the sanding process before building the project, especially if you're considering using power tools.

Other Tools and Accessories

In addition to the foregoing tools that perform the major tasks in woodworking, other tools and accessories may be useful in making the projects. For example, if you do not have a workbench or a place to build one, consider buying one (Illus. 37). These compact but functional devices are very useful where there is not much space for doing woodworking. Many of these units fold up and can be tucked away.

If you want to make sawhorses for your shop or work area, consider using commercially available metal brackets (Illus. 38). Sturdy and functional sawhorses can be quickly made of 2 × 4's from

Illus. 37. Workbench (photo courtesy of Black & Decker ®).

19

Illus. 38. Sawhorse brackets (photo courtesy of Stanley Tools).

Illus. 39. Utility knife (photo courtesy of Stanley Tools).

Illus. 40. Hobby knife (photo courtesy of Stanley Tools).

When cutting metal, you may find a hacksaw (Illus. 41) useful. One of the projects involves cutting brass tubing. A hacksaw would be the tool of choice for such a project. If you decide to make mirrors as a gift project, you will need a standard and, if desired, a circle glass cutter. Another option is to order the glass from the local glass store.

There are a variety of clamps of different types and sizes that you will find helpful when making the projects. One clamp that comes in a variety of sizes is the C-clamp (Illus. 42). As the need

Illus. 41. Hacksaw (photo courtesy of Stanley Tools).

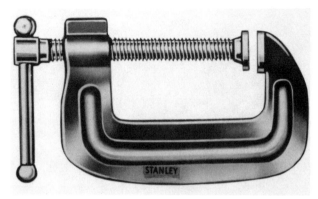

Illus. 42. C-clamp (photo courtesy of Stanley Tools).

arises, shop the local stores and the mail-order suppliers for clamps. They can be critical when you are gluing and assembling some of the projects.

A hammer is needed to assemble many of the projects. Also of use is a nail set (Illus. 43). Available in different sizes, a nail set permits you to drive the heads of finishing nails below the wood's surface. While not a mandatory item, the nail set makes the surface of a project look neater.

Illus. 43. Nail set (photo courtesy of Stanley Tools).

WOOD, SUPPLIES, AND FINISHING PRODUCTS

Wood

Once you encounter the smell of a freshly cut piece of pine or oak, you will want to become a woodworker. When you do work with wood, however, be certain to put on a dust mask to minimize the amount of wood dust you will inhale. There are a variety of dust masks and related devices that you should purchase and use when working with wood.

While most of the projects can be made from pine, some require the use of hardwoods. Wood is generally termed either a hardwood or a softwood. These designations, however, are often misleading. For example, some hardwoods are soft, and some softwoods are hard. Wood-carvers like to use basswood, which is a hardwood but in fact is very soft. Despite these seeming contradictions, the wood industry continues to use these terms.

Actually, the distinction between hardwoods and softwoods is based on some rather technical factors. As a general guideline, hardwoods come from trees that shed their leaves and are called *deciduous*. For example, walnut, maple, oak, cherry, birch, and many other trees that you're familiar with are considered hardwoods. Trees that have needles all year around, called *conifers*, are generally considered softwoods. This group includes the pines, spruce, fir, and other evergreens that are used by the wood industry.

Another difference between the two basic wood groups is price. As a rule, the hardwoods are more expensive than the softwoods. The softwoods are readily available at various sources in your community, while the hardwoods may be hard to find. In most communities, a quick look in the Yellow Pages or a similar directory will indicate if there are any hardwood dealers in the area. Given the general interest in woodworking, many cities have several hardwood dealers. Hardwoods can also be found at the large do-it-yourself stores, or ordered from many mail-order suppliers. Again, an excellent source of information is the various national woodworking magazines.

For those beginning woodworkers, it should be noted that hardwoods can be more difficult to work with, especially if you do not have floor-model power tools. While hardwoods should be used for most of the wood-turning projects, pine may be the preferable wood for other projects. An exception to this would be the carving projects. For most of these projects use basswood, one of the soft hardwoods.

If you're new to woodworking, try working with the different woods. Learn about these woods and their various properties, and then determine what kinds of woods to use in the gift projects.

When you shop for your project wood, take along a tape measure. Also have a general idea of how much wood you will need. Where possible, pick out your own boards. If you're looking for pine, buy what is called by lumber graders No. 3 common. This is the most readily available grade of pine, and is generally used in the house construction industry. It is the least expensive and lends itself to crafting.

Avoid boards with loose knots, dripping sap, or resin. While knots are always present in this grade of lumber, pick boards where they are tightly in place. Avoid boards that are warped or twisted. Sight down the length of the board to be certain that it's relatively straight.

When you order wood, you should be aware of

the differences between its stated and actual dimensions. For example, a 1 x 4-inch pine board is not 1 inch thick and 4 inches wide. These dimensions are the rough-cut or nominal size of the board. The board is actually ¾-inch thick and 3½ inches wide. These dimensions are the true or planed sizes of the board. Here is another example. A 2 x 4-inch stud, commonly used in house construction, is in fact 1½ inches thick and 3½ inches wide.

In most instances, you can rely on the stated length of a board. An 8-foot, 1-inch x 4-inch board will be 8 feet long. When measuring and laying out projects, allow for differences in the thicknesses and widths of the boards.

A totally different grading and measuring system is used on hardwoods. When shopping for hardwoods, ask the dealer for information on how hardwoods are graded and measured. Don't hesitate to admit your ignorance. Most dealers are delighted to explain this grading and measuring system to perspective customers. Take advantage of their expertise.

For some projects, hardwoods can be obtained from the backyard wood pile. If you want to turn weed pots, find oak or some other hardwood that's been lying on the wood pile for several years. Fireplace wood can be used to carve some projects, especially small birds. A slice of log makes an excellent base for the several shorebird and other gift projects. This is an inexpensive way to get hardwoods.

Another source of hardwoods is pallets or other types of packing or shipping devices. Usually, they are made from hardwood that, after you have removed the nails, can be used for making projects. Plants or factories in your community can be a source for pallets.

One type of hardwood not mentioned is what generally is called the exotics or imports. As a rule, these woods are more expensive because they are in limited supply and also because they must be imported. Some of the exotics are from Africa, while many are from South and Central America. As you may know, there is great concern about the ongoing devastation of the rain forests around the world. Many woodworkers are refusing to buy the exotics to both protest and hopefully stop the devastation of the forests.

There are many other things that you will learn and will want to learn about wood once you start making the projects. You will also find yourself more interested in trees and, oddly enough, the environment in general. There are some excellent books available on wood and trees that you should consult for more information.

Supplies

There are a variety of supplies that will help you in making your gift projects. Some of these items are necessary to the actual crafting of the projects. Others are items that either enhance a project or make crafting it a lot easier.

For assembling the gift projects, you will need a bottle of wood glue. While there are a number of excellent types available, buy yellow wood glue. For some tasks, a container of white glue will be useful. As with any product, read the label directions prior to use.

When nails or screws are not used in assembling a project, use clamps to hold the glued pieces in place until they are dry. The C-clamps mentioned earlier can be used. So can bar clamps.

In addition to wood glue, you will need finishing nails and wire brads of various sizes. The best approach to buying what is needed is to familiarize yourself with what's available in the local hardware store. The nail set mentioned earlier will prove useful when you seat both finishing nails and brads.

Some projects will require the use of wood screws, along with glue. Wood screws have an extruded thread and are easy to use. Some of the drywall screws on the market will prove useful. The specific sizes of screws, finishing nails, and brads required for a project are stated in the project directions.

Standard dowels, available in most hardware stores, are used in several projects. In some instances, rather than buying commercial pegs, you may want to make your own from dowels. One project has instructions for using walnut dowels, which can be purchased at hardwood dealers or from mail-order suppliers. You may want to locate several sources that you can purchase dowels from for the gift projects.

Some projects require that you use components that can only be provided by a commercial supplier. For example, a desktop clock, shaped from a piece of spalted hardwood, utilizes a small digital clock movement inserted into the wood. Numerous mail-order suppliers offer a variety of clocks in all sizes and with a range of prices.

Another project features a round, marble cutting piece secured to a shaped, hard-maple cutting board. The marble is available from a mail-order supplier and is reasonably priced. Desktop pen sets utilize ballpoint pens and funnels purchased from a mail-order supplier.

Shaker pegs, candle cups, toy wheels and axles, cup pegs, key-rack pegs, tie pegs, wooden checkers, and other parts are used in the various projects. These parts are also available through mail-order suppliers. Sheets of cork for message or bulletin boards, along with pre-cut round cork inserts for drink coasters, are also available through the mail. You will find that when reviewing supplies that are available, new project ideas will emerge, along with different ways to enhance your gift projects.

It should be noted, again, that there are many gift projects that do not utilize any commercial supplies. You have lots of options to select from as you plan your gift making. If you prefer using the various commercial supplies, you may want to further enhance some gift projects. Examine the various mail-order catalogues to see what's available. There is a considerable variety of interesting items, both in terms of quality and price. For example, you can purchase a gold pen and funnel, as opposed to plastic ones. The products are there if you're inclined to spend the money.

Finishing Products

The finishing process, in some ways, is more important than the gift-making process. A poor finishing job attracts attention and distracts from an otherwise well-made project. In most instances,

a poorly finished project is the result of haste, using the wrong finishing products, or not reading or following the product label directions. Take the finishing process seriously. If not, the end result will be a disastrous project. The basic information about finishing techniques and the various products available that are presented here may help you avoid any problems.

When you explore the paint department in a hardware store, it will seem overwhelming. Modern chemistry has done wonders in making available such a wide variety of finishing products to the consumer. Most manufacturers, however, provide detailed product information, presented in a way that the average consumer can understand. Much of it will clarify what the product is for, how to use it, what kind of brush to use with it, and even how to clean it up after use.

An additional resource that you should exploit is an informed clerk or owner. Take advantage of the expertise that they have. This is an excellent place and way to begin learning about how best to finish your gift projects.

Finishing products generally fall into two groups. One group consists of all those products that are absorbed into the wood. The other group of products are those that remain on the surface of the wood. The decision on which group of products to use is based more on personal preference than anything else. Products that remain on the surface are generally the lacquers, the polyurethanes, the varnishes, and various types of paint. On projects where a clear, hard finish is desired, I like to use Deft, a lacquer. It not only dries quickly, but leaves a nice semi-gloss finish that can be further rubbed down with steel wool (0000).

The only downside to Deft and other finishing products is that you have to work with them in a well-ventilated area. Carefully read and follow the directions on these finishing products.

Deft is an excellent finish to use on the various hardwood projects. It also works well on pine, whether stained or natural. Deft is best applied with a good-quality brush. Inexpensive brushes tend to leave brush hair and other marks on the finished surface.

Many of the projects will be painted or decorated with paint. Most of the pine projects are painted. There are numerous paint colors available that give projects an Americana appearance. Many of the latex gloss enamels work well on pine, but you may want to first use a sealer or a primer coat. Here, again, both the paint store literature and the label directions on the can will be most helpful.

Latex gloss enamel paint can be cleaned from the brushes with soap and water. These paints are also available in a variety of colors. They can be used to either paint the project or to give detail to it. Have some small brushes available so that you can embellish the projects when desired.

When painting a project, especially birds, remember that you are only approximating the way they look. You will have a great deal of fun painting and detailing your gift projects.

Products that are absorbed by the wood make up the second major group of finishing products. Some woodworkers prefer these kinds of finishes over the surface ones. There are many types of oil that can be used to finish wood items. One that I prefer is Watco Danish Oil that is natural in color. While the product is available in some colors, the natural color doesn't change, but only enhances the natural appearance and color of the wood. As with any finishing product, read the label warnings and directions before using it.

Mineral oil works well on cutting boards. It is a pure oil that both preserves and makes the wood more attractive. Some oils are toxic, and should not be used on projects that will be used with food. Other oils tend to turn rancid. Before applying mineral oil to the wood, warm the wood by a heat outlet. The wood will absorb the oil better. Periodically reoil cutting boards. The oil tends to leave the wood when the wood is used and cleaned.

Oil- or water-based stains are another product that is absorbed into the wood. For some projects, I use an oil-based Danish walnut stain. I apply and wipe the stain off with a rag. When it is dry, I apply several coats of Deft to the surface.

As a rule, cover the stained item with a surface finish. As with all products, read the label prior to buying and using the stains. Rub several coats of a paste wax on projects that will receive a lot of wear or are subject to dust accumulation. For example, shelves that are stained and lacquered should be rubbed with a paste wax.

BEFORE YOU BEGIN

The following projects are presented randomly. This approach will expose you to the diversity of gifts that can be made, and confronts you with possibilities for crafting that you may not otherwise consider. When projects are presented according to tools or methods to be used, there is a tendency to consider only those projects that are similar to ones done before.

In addition to a photograph of each gift project, a list of materials is presented. The material list is simply a guideline and does not have to be followed exactly. For example, where the list may suggest using pine, you may decide to use one of the hardwoods. You may also have a different idea on which other materials to use. The list also suggests a possible finish to use. Again, you may prefer a totally different finish.

When appropriate, a dimensional drawing of a project is also presented. For some gift projects, you may want to modify these dimensions. For example, you may want a longer or wider shelf than the one presented in the project drawing. Much of the fun in making gifts is to craft them in your own unique way and in sizes that suit your needs.

In some instances, tools available may dictate the size of a project. Be willing to modify the size of the project by using different designs and dimensions.

Each project also has a suggested list of tools to use. If you lack a particular tool and don't want to buy one, you may have to improvise. Much of the fun in doing woodworking is to discover different ways to maximize the use of a tool. As you review a particular project, you may know of a way to achieve the same results, but with different methods and tools.

Specific instructions are provided for each gift project. In a step-by-step manner, they tell you how to make the gift project. To minimize repetition of some detailed instructions, they will be given only once. For example, instructions on how to set up and use a table-mounted router for a project will be given once. Other projects that require using the same tool will have a reference to the earlier project.

While you may want to follow project directions exactly as given, you may also decide to add some steps of your own. This is encouraged. It's thrilling to utilize your own ideas and methods to make a gift. Let the directions serve only as guidelines as you explore the woodworking process.

Michael D. Berger
1025 Calle Pecos
Thousand Oaks, CA 91360

PROJECTS

1: Desktop Pen-and-Paper-Clip Set (Illus. 44 and 45)

This pen-and-paper-clip set, made from hardwood scrap, is an attractive, functional, and easy-to-make desktop piece. The desktop set shown in Illus. 44 is made from red oak. The base contains a turned paper-clip storage area that could be eliminated if desired. The size and shape of the base, especially if scrap material is used, presents you with an opportunity to be creative and to personalize the gift. A variety of pens and holders are available for easy attachment to the crafted base.

MATERIAL:
- 1″ (4/4's) thick piece of scrap hardwood
- Pen set
- Lacquer for finishing

TOOLS:
- Sabre saw or band saw
- Electric drill and bits (3/8″ and 1/8″)
- Wood lathe and roundnose scraper

OPTIONAL TOOLS:
- Drill press
- 2″ or larger multi-spur bit

DIRECTIONS:
1. Determine the size and type of base desired. Consider using a piece of scrap hardwood if it is available. Look for a piece with unusual wood grain, bark, or color, so that it will stand out on a desk. Saw it to the desired dimensions.
2. If you want a turned storage area for paper clips, mount a pine glue block, off-center, on the bottom of the base. This placement of the glue block will result in the paper-clip area being off-center when turned. Secure a faceplate to the glue block, mount the glue block to the lathe, and turn the clip area at least 1/2″ deep and with a diameter of at least 2 7/8″. A roundnose scraper works well for turning this area.
3. If you want a paper-clip area but don't have a lathe, drill a hole using a drill press and a 2″ or larger multi-spur bit. The drilled hole should be at least 1/2″ deep. In that the bit leaves an unsightly surface at the bottom of the hole, glue a piece of brown or green felt onto the surface, after the piece has been finished.
4. Using fine and extra-fine abrasive paper, prepare the base for finishing. Be sure to sand with the wood grain. Remove the sharp edges on both the top and bottom of the base, using abrasive paper.
5. Purchase a variety of pens with funnels and attaching devices from local craft stores or mail-

Illus. 44. Desktop pen-and-paper-clip set.

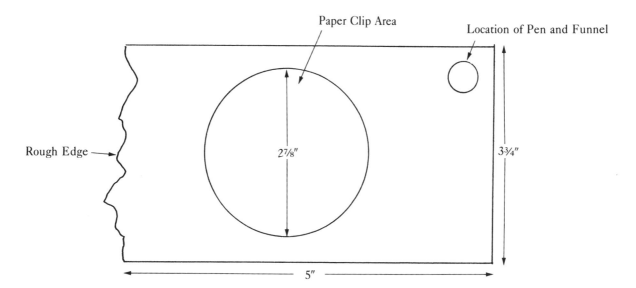

Paper Clip Area

Location of Pen and Funnel

Rough Edge

2⅞″

3¾″

5″

Illus. 45. Drawing of desktop pen-and-paper-clip set.

order suppliers. The pens are available in different finishes and prices. It's best to purchase a pen in which the actual writing device can be replaced.

6. Secure the pen and its holder to the top surface of the base. Specific instructions usually accompany the pen and holder. While some woodworkers secure the pen and holder to the base surface, others drill a hole through the base to accommodate a screw. Usually a ⅜″ diameter hole will accommodate the screw head, and a ⅛″ diameter hole the shaft. If the recipient is right-handed, place the pen and holder in the upper right-hand corner. The opposite placement is usually acceptable for the left-handed writer. If a paper-clip area has been turned or drilled, placement of the pen should be done in relation to this area.

7. Finish the desk set with a clear lacquer. If you prefer a softer looking finish, use one of the oil finishes. Read and follow label directions carefully on all finishing products. To avoid scratching the desk top, place round felt dots on the bottom surface. Felt dots can be purchased or cut from a scrap piece of felt.

8. A brass presentation plate can be purchased and engraved with an appropriate message. The plate can be attached to the top surface or the front edge.

2. *Rectangular Mirror*

(Illus. 46 and 47)

Mirrors are highly prized gifts, especially if they are crafted from walnut or some other hardwood. So, while this mirror can also be made from pine, if you have access to hardwood and have the needed tools, use it. The mirror shown in Illus. 46 is made of black walnut and has an oil finish. Given the mirror's size, it is more decorative than functional. You may want to enlarge it while retaining the rectangular shape. Instructions on cutting mirror glass are provided with the directions. You can, of course, purchase the mirror to size at a local glass dealer.

MATERIAL:
- Black walnut 6″ wide, 12″ long, 1″ thick (approximate)
- Mirror
- Wood glue and white glue
- Rubber bands (No. 105: 5″ long, ⅝″ wide)
- Construction paper
- Mineral oil

TOOLS:
- Band or table saw

Illus. 46. *Rectangular mirror.*

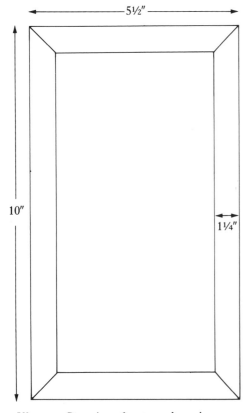

Illus. 47. *Drawing of rectangular mirror.*

- Mitre saw
- Table-mounted router and bits (roundover and rabbeting)
- Glass cutter

DIRECTIONS:

1. If you're using the suggested dimensions, cut three strips approximately 1 ¼″ wide and 12″ long. Before sawing and mitring the various pieces, do the routing. It's safer and easier this way. Follow all safety procedures when using power tools.

2. The first routing task is to cut a rabbet in the edge of the pieces to accommodate the mirror. Set the rabbeting bit to cut a depth of at least ⅛″. Most mirror glass that you buy and cut yourself is approximately ³⁄₁₆″ thick. If you plan to use thicker glass, cut the rabbet deeper. Before routing, examine the surfaces of the three pieces. Select the best surface for the front of the mirror. Make the rabbet cuts on its bottom edge.

3. Using a roundover bit secured in the mounted router, rout all remaining edges. Do not, of course, rout the rabbeted edge. After setting the bit, rout a piece of scrap to be certain that the bit is set properly. The edges should be only slightly rounded.

4. Depending upon the type of mitre saw to be used, set it to cut at 45 degrees. Make sure that the rabbeted edges will be on the inside bottom surface of each piece, and then cut the strips to length. Make sure that the two side pieces are exactly the same length. Also make sure that the top and bottom pieces are exactly the same length. Before making each cut, check to see that it is correct. Mitring can be confusing, so take your time. Remember to follow all safety procedures.

5. While frames for gluing together mitres are available, rubber bands work well. You need a flat surface with a block clamped or nailed to it, so that you can force the frame against the block as you slip the rubber band around the frame. With two rubber bands close at hand, spread wood glue on all joint surfaces. Assemble the frame and, while holding it together with your hands, slide it into the block. Place the rubber band over the frame edge nearest to you and stretch it so that it surrounds all edges. The clamped block holds the assembled frame in place while you are stretching the rubber band around it.

After the rubber band is in place, if necessary, realign each mitre. The rubber-band method puts equal pressure on all joints. You may want to slip a second rubber band over it to put slightly more pressure on the joints.

Wipe off any excess glue that may have been squeezed from the joints. Leave the rubber bands in place until the glue dries.

6. Using fine-grit abrasive paper, prepare all surfaces for finishing. Be certain to sand with the grain, especially around the joints.

7. Wipe off all dust prior to finishing. If an oil finish is desired, read the product label directions and proceed accordingly. If you prefer a lacquer finish, rub the surface between coats, with the grain, using extra-fine steel wool (0000). Wipe off the dust and wool hairs prior to applying another coat of lacquer.

8. While you can measure the inside area of the frame and have a local glass store cut the mirror, you may want to cut your own. If so, purchase mirror tiles which are generally 12″ × 12″ square. At the same time, buy a glass cutter. In addition to the glass cutter, a steel ruler with a rubber-type backing is needed.

Measure and cut the mirror so that it is slightly smaller than the actual inside dimensions of the rabbeted area of the frame. This will eliminate any possibility of an over-sized mirror that has to be chipped along its edges to fit the frame. While the mirror can be measured with the small indentations on the glass cutter, there is a much better method. Using an alcohol pen and a ruler, mark the size needed on the mirror's reflective surface. With the ruler aligned on the inside of the line, run the glass cutter, applying even pressure on it, down and along the side of the ruler. Cut the full length of the mirror tile, even though there will be some waste. Align the scratch made by the cutter, face-up, on the sharp edge of a bench or board. While holding the mirror in place with one hand, press down on the section extending over the board or bench with the other

hand. The mirror should crack, evenly, along the line. Repeat the process to cut along the other dimensional line.

9. Place the mirror into the rabbeted area of the frame and spread white glue on the corner edges and along the sides. When the glue is dry, the mirror will be secured into the frame. Don't use too much glue, as it will squeeze out on the front surface of the mirror.

10. Measure and cut a piece of construction paper that will cover the back of the frame. Glue it in place.

11. Drill a small hole into the back center of the top piece of the frame, in which to hang the mirror. Be careful not to drill through the frame. An alternative is to use one of the many hanging devices that are available and can be nailed to the back of the frame. If using these devices, be very careful when hammering, so that the mirror is not broken.

3: *Leaf Press* (Illus. 48 and 49)

This leaf press is both fun to make and instructive for those who use it. Colorful fall leaves can be drilled and preserved in this press. It's a simple device to use, so it makes an especially good gift for children. It's also an excellent way to learn how to identify leaves or use them for decorations.

MATERIAL:
• ¼″ thick external plywood
• ¼″ diameter bolts and wing nuts
• Washers
• Cardboard
• Paint

TOOLS:
• Sabre or band saw
• Electric drill and bit (¼″)

DIRECTIONS:
1. Measure and cut two pieces of plywood to the desired dimensions.
2. Using cardboard boxes or a similar source, cut

Illus. 48. Leaf press.

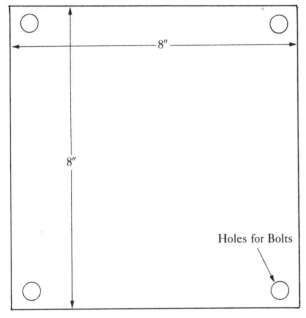

Illus. 49. Drawing of leaf press.

four pieces of cardboard the same size as the plywood. A utility knife and a metal ruler can be used to cut cardboard well. Since the leaves are placed between the layers of cardboard for drying and pressing, you may also want to use construction paper between the cardboard and the leaves.
3. Measure and drill holes at the corners, through the plywood and cardboard. The diameter of the holes must accommodate the bolts. The bolts must be long enough to penetrate the

plywood and cardboard and still have sufficient length for two washers and a wing nut.

After placing the leaves between the layers of cardboard, insert the bolts, a washer on each side, and then thread and tighten the wing nut. This puts pressure on both presses and dries the leaves. The leaves should remain under pressure for several days.
4. Paint and decorate the plywood. Try using one of the many stencils that are on the market.

4: *Shorebird 1* (Illus. 50 and 51)

This is the first of several shorebirds that are presented for you to shape and carve. Unlike many carved birds, the shorebird in this project is an approximation of the real bird. While you may want to paint or wood-burn some details on the project, it is not necessary. You can use a dowel for the bill or beak, a nail for the eye, and a clear lacquer for the finish.

MATERIAL:
- 3″ (12/4's) thick basswood
- ¼″ diameter dowel
- ⅛″ diameter dowel
- Chunk of firewood

TOOLS:
- Band saw
- Electric grinder
- Large tungsten carbide burrs
- Carving or sloyd knife
- Electric drill and bits (¼″ and ¼″)
- Electric finishing sander

DIRECTIONS:
1. Use either a self-made pattern from construction paper or draw the shorebird outline to size on the surface of the basswood. If basswood is not available, glue together two pieces of 2″ × 6″ pine to use for the bird. Try to use pieces that have no or a minimum of knots. Clamp the two pieces together until the glue dries.
2. Using a ¼″ wide blade on a band saw, cut the traced shorebird from the block. If you're

Illus. 50. Shorebird I.

skilled with a band saw, you may want to do some initial shaping of the bird. Work carefully.

3. With the sloyd or carving knife, remove wood, with the grain, and cut the bird's rough shape. Use the knife very carefully, as it is usually extremely sharp. Review Illus. 50 as you carve the bird to shape.

4. Using the electric grinder and a large carbide burr, do the final shaping. The burr removes wood very quickly, so it is easy to clean up the knife and saw marks and shape the bird. An apron and a mask are necessary when using the grinder and burr, which create a lot of sawdust. Again, as with any tool, use the grinder and burr carefully. Read and follow the tool directions. You may want to clamp the block onto a workbench while grinding on it.

5. Use the electric finishing sander, with 100-grit abrasive paper, to remove markings from the burr and do any final shaping. The sander can be

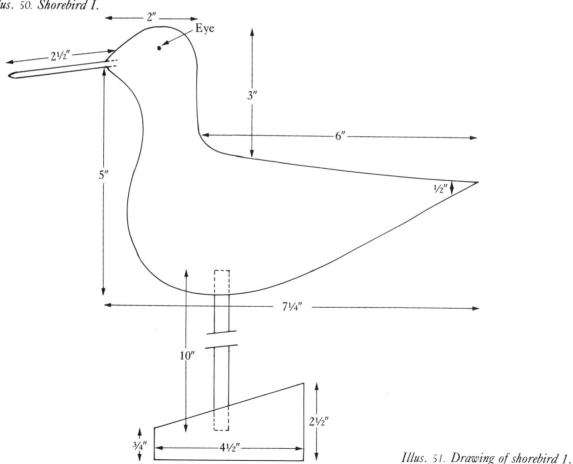

Illus. 51. Drawing of shorebird 1.

31

very helpful in finalizing the shape of the neck and head area. If you prefer, use an 80-grit abrasive paper to remove the wood more quickly. Prepare the surface of the bird for finishing using the sander and a series of fine-grit abrasive papers. Sand with the wood grain to eliminate scratches.

6. Approximate the location of the eyes and make holes using a nail or punch.

7. Cut a block from the chunk of firewood. The block will serve as a support base for displaying the shorebird. Be certain it's large enough and won't permit the bird to tip over.

8. In the bottom center of the bird, drill a ¼" diameter hole that will receive the ¼" support dowel. The hole should be at least ¾" deep. Drill another hole, ¾" deep, in the top center of the support base.

9. Cut a 10" length of ¼" dowel. Insert the dowel into the bird and base. Do not glue these parts, as you may want to, on occasion, take the bird and base apart.

10. Drill a ⅛" diameter hole about ½" deep where the bill should protrude from the head.

11. Measure and cut a 2½" piece of ⅛" diameter dowel. Sand one end to a point, so that it resembles a bird bill. Spread a small amount of wood glue on the opposite end and insert it into the drilled hole.

12. Finish the bird, base, and dowels with several coats of lacquer. Rub the surface, between coats, with extra-fine steel wool (0000). Add a final coat of paste wax and polish the surface with a soft rag. This will add a very attractive finish to the project.

5: Wooden Dish (Illus. 52 and 53)

This is a functional and attractive gift, especially when turned from black walnut or a similar domestic hardwood. If desired, you can turn it to a specific diameter for use in a special place. The project, as you might guess, is turned on a lathe using a faceplate.

MATERIAL:

- Black walnut 1¼" (5/4's) thick, 9½" wide, and 9½" long
- Pine glue block

TOOLS:

- Band or sabre saw
- Wood lathe
- 3" faceplate
- Roundnose scraper or bowl gouge

DIRECTIONS:

1. Using a school compass, draw a pattern for the largest circle possible for a turning block. Cut the bock using either a band or sabre saw. Try to keep the block perfectly round when cutting so that when it is on the lathe, it will be easier to turn.

2. Cut a 4" diameter pine glue block from 1" thick stock.

3. Spread white glue on the pine block and the center bottom surface of the turning block. Place the glue block on the exact center of the turning block, using the indentation made by the compass point as a guide. If possible, clamp the two pieces together until the glue is dry. You may have to place some heavy object on the glue block if you don't have a sufficiently large clamp.

4. Center a 3" faceplate on the glue block and secure the block with wood screws. Mount it on the lathe.

5. Depending upon whether you prefer the scraping or cutting method of turning, select a tool and shape the outer surface of the block.

Illus. 52. Wooden dish.

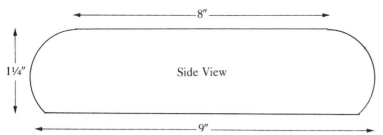

8"

Side View

1¼"

9"

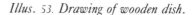

Give it a rolled appearance, as indicated in both Illus. 52 and 53.

6. Realign the tool rest and turn the inside of the dish. Turn the inside edge concave, to conform with the outside edge of the dish. Flatten the bottom, but make sure that it rolls as it approaches the concave edge.

7. If necessary, prepare the surface for finishing using fine-grit abrasive paper and extra-fine steel wool (0000).

8. Unless you prefer to finish the piece on the lathe, remove the glue block from the bottom surface. Either cut it off using a band saw or chisel it off. Take your time, to ensure that you don't damage the turned dish. Sand away any glue that remains on the bottom surface and prepare the piece for finishing.

9. Apply either a lacquer or oil finish, depending upon your preference.

6: *Fish Decoys* (Illus. 54 and 55)

This gift can be displayed individually, as a hanging school of fish, or as a mobile. For those giving the gift to a fisherman, the fish can be hung with a self-made wire hook through the mouth. Using nylon string and a few small brads, you can hang fish in a swimming position. As with any school of fish, the fish vary greatly in size. Make them to any length, width, or shape desired.

MATERIAL:
- ½" thick pine
- Thin aluminum sheets (scraps from a print shop)
- Nylon fish line
- Small brads
- Red and white paint

TOOLS:
- Sabre or scroll saw
- Electric finishing sander
- Hobby knife (pointed blade)
- Scissors (kitchen-style)

DIRECTIONS:
1. Design and make fish patterns from construction or heavy scrap paper. Draw the fish to the size and shape desired. Cut out the patterns. Use your imagination and be creative with the designs.

Illus. 54. *Fish decoys.*

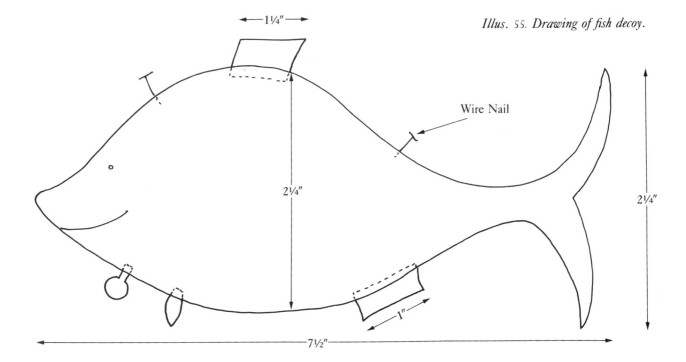

1¼"

2¼"

Wire Nail

2¼"

1"

7½"

2. Trace the patterns on the surface of the ½" thick pine boards with the wood grain. Cut out the fish using a scroll or sabre saw. Cut a mouth, appropriately placed, on each fish.

3. Using the electric sander and coarse-grit abrasive paper, shape the fish. As with a real fish, the top and bottom edges should be narrow, and the center area thick. The front mouth area should be thin, as should portions of the tail. Again, be creative and make the fish resemble what you perceive a fish to look like.

4. Draw the various fins required for the fish freehand on the aluminum sheets. If you can't find aluminum, use either tin or brass sheets that can be purchased at local hardware stores. Use an alcohol pen to draw the fins on the surface of the metal. The traced fins can be cut out with a kitchen-type scissors. The fins should be shaped in relation to where they will be placed on the fish. Note Illus. 54 and 55. Placement of the fins also determines the size of the fish. Allow an extra ⅛" on the bottom of each fin so that it can be glued into slots that will be cut into the edges of the fish.

5. Using a hobby knife with a pointed blade, cut slots in the top and bottom edges of each fish where the fins are to be placed. Be careful when using this type of knife and making this kind of cut. Take your time. You may want to secure the fish in a small vise or clamp it to a workbench when making the fin cuts. The slots should be at least ⅛" deep.

6. Apply a bead of white glue to the bottom edge of each fin and force them into the appropriate slots. Wipe off any excess glue from the fins or the wood's surface. Be careful not to cut your fingers on the sharp edges or corners of the fins. You may want to wear a leather glove when forcing the fins in place.

7. For hanging your fish, place two small brads on the top edge of the fish. Use nylon fish line for hanging. If you prefer the "caught look," make a small fish hook from wire; make sure that it has an eye for the line. Drill a hole through the mouth area to accommodate the hook, thread the line through the hook's eye, and hang the fish. If you want to make a mobile, use pieces of ⅛" diameter dowels and nylon line.

8. Using red paint and a fine brush, paint the fins. If you prefer, paint the fish white or leave it natural. Paint a red dot on each side for eyes. Don't hesitate to do other decorations on the fish.

7: *Cattails* (Illus. 56 and 57)

For those who would like to have a vase of cattails throughout the year, this is the ideal gift. When turned from black walnut, it's hard to tell these cattails from the real things. If you are willing to buy 1″ diameter black walnut dowels, this project can be made without a lathe. For the turner, however, this is a fun project that can be quickly and easily made in quantity. And best of all, the seed pods on these cattails won't break and spread white-tailed seeds all over the house.

MATERIAL:
- 1¼″ (5/4's) thick walnut
- ¼″ diameter dowels

TOOLS:
- Band, table, or radial arm saw
- Wood lathe and roundnose scraper
- Electric drill and bit (¼″)

DIRECTIONS:
1. Measure and cut black-walnut turning blanks that are at least 4½″ long and 1¼″ (5/4's) thick and wide. It's easier and less wasteful if the blanks are square.

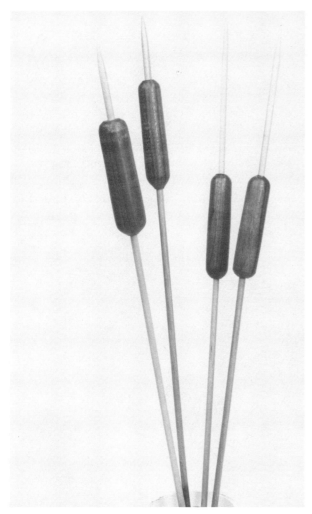

Illus. 56. Cattails.

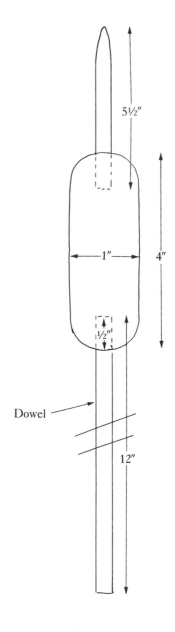

Illus. 57. Drawing of Cattail.

2. Use a ball-bearing center in the tailstock of the lathe, and a spur drive in the headstock. If you have a collet or some other type of chuck system, use it.

3. Mark the center point on both ends of the blank and place the blank between the centers. Review Illus. 56 and 57 to note how the ends of the pods are to be shaped. Using either a round-nose scraper or a gouge of choice, turn the pod to shape it. Repeat the process until all the blanks have been turned.

4. Drill ¼″ diameter holes approximately ½″ deep in both ends of the pods. Use the marks from the lathe centers to determine the midpoint where the holes are to be drilled.

5. Cut ¼″ diameter dowels to varying lengths for insertion into the top and bottom of the pods. The bottom piece should be approximately 12″ long, and the top section 5½″ long.

6. Sand the top end of the dowels to a point, to resemble an actual cattail. Place wood glue in the drilled holes in the seed pod and insert the dowels. Allow the glue to dry.

7. Use lacquer to finish the cattails.

8: *Elephant Pull Toy* (Illus.

58 and 59)

The elephant is always a popular creature to model toys after. It lends itself to many different shapes, designs, and sizes. Put a board and wheels under a few elephants, add a trailer, and you have a marvellous pull toy. Don't forget to add a string with a small elephant attached to it to make pulling the toy easier.

MATERIAL:
- 1″ × 8″ pine
- 1″ × 4″ pine
- 2″ diameter wheels with axles
- 1″ diameter wheels with axles
- Eye screws
- String
- Red, yellow, and black paint

TOOLS:
- Sabre or scroll saw
- Electric drill and bit (¼″)
- Finishing sander

DIRECTIONS:
1. Using construction paper, make patterns of the three different sizes of elephants. Refer to Illus. 58 and 59 if you need guidance. It's much easier to make elephants of the same design and size when you use patterns.

2. Trace the large elephant pattern onto the surface of 1″ × 8″ pine. Trace the remaining elephants on a 1″ × 4″ pine board. Place and trace the patterns with the wood grain. You

Illus. 58. Elephant pull toy.

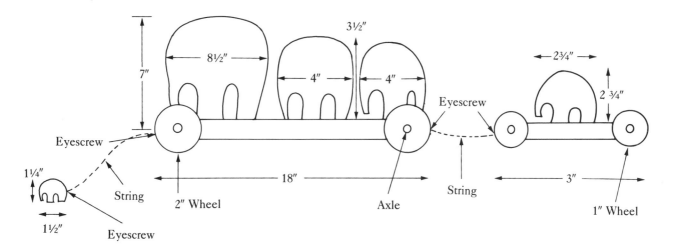

Illus. 59. Drawing of elephant pull toy.

should also place the bottom of the elephants' feet on the edge of the board. This will give you a flat, square surface for the feet.

3. Using either a sabre or scroll saw, cut out the traced elephants.

4. Measure and cut the large trailer board from a piece of 1″ × 4″ stock. As Illus. 59 indicates, it's 18″ long and 3½″ wide, the exact width of a 1″ × 4″. Measure and cut out the smaller trailer. It should be 3″ long and approximately 2½″ wide.

5. Using a ruler, measure and mark the points where the wheel-axle holes should be drilled on both trailers. Drill the holes, using a ¼″ diameter bit for ¼″ diameter axles. Make sure that the holes are drilled straight, or the wheels will rub on the trailer.

6. Do not assemble the toy until after all the parts have been painted. The toy shown in Illus. 58 has elephants that are painted red, trailers that are yellow, and wheels that are black. The head of the axles on the large trailer are yellow, and black on the small trailer. Use your imagination when painting the toy. Make it bright and cheerful, to attract the attention of a child, young or old.

7. Spread wood glue on the feet of the elephants and place them on the trailers. Refer to Illus. 58 for placement ideas. In addition to the glue, you may want to secure the elephants in place by driving a small finishing nail through the trailer and into the feet of each elephant.

8. Place a spot of glue in the axle holes, slip the axles through the wheels, and tap the assembly in place. Make sure that the wheels rotate freely.

9. Secure small eye screws to the front and back of the large trailer, one to the front of the small trailer, and, of course, one to the back area of the elephant being pulled.

10. Thread a strong string through all the eye screws. Have fun!

9: *Elephant Cutting Board* (Illus. 60 and 61)

No doubt elephants will continue to be popular in this country for many years to come. This popularity is not only of a political nature, but also of a zoological one. People love these large, wonderful critters and enjoy seeing them at the zoo. What better gift is there to give an elephant lover than a hard-maple cutting board, designed to resemble one of these creatures?

MATERIAL:
- 1″ (4/4's) thick hard maple
- Mineral oil

TOOLS:
- Band, scroll, or sabre saw
- Table-mounted router and roundover bit

Illus. 60. Elephant cutting board.

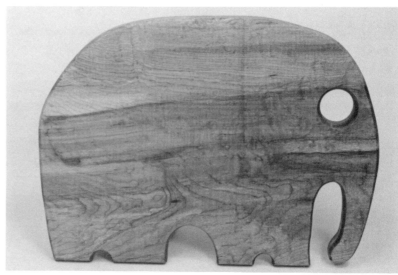

Illus. 61. Drawing of elephant cutting board.

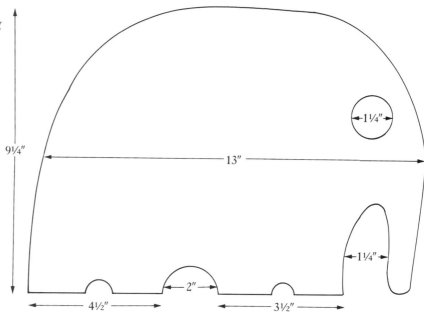

• Finishing sander

DIRECTIONS:

1. Design and cut a pattern from construction paper. Duplicate the suggested dimensions for the project or reduce or enlarge them. In part, this will depend on the type of wood that's available. Hard maple is the wood of choice for a cutting board, but oak or one of the other hardwoods can be used.

2. Trace the pattern onto the surface of the wood with the grain.

3. Cut out the pattern using one of the suggested saws. If a band saw is used, you will need a ⅛″ wide blade. If you use a sabre saw or a floor-model scroll saw, use a blade that will cut hardwood.

4. If you want to cut an eye in the cutting board, you will need a drill press and a 1¼″ diameter multi-spur bit. A smaller eye can be drilled with an electric drill and a wood bit. The eye can also be used for hanging the cutting board.

5. Using a table-mounted router and a round-over bit, rout all edges on both sides of the board. If a large eye has been drilled, this should also be routed.

6. Apply several coats of mineral oil to all surfaces. The oil is absorbed better if the wood is warm.

10: *Loon* (Illus. 62 and 63)

The distinct sound a loon makes, its ability to dive under water, and the way it looks make it an easily recognized and much-loved part of our environment. A loon crafted and painted by you will be a much appreciated and prominently displayed gift. Designed to suggest that the loon is sitting on the water, this project is quick and easy to make and decorate.

MATERIAL:
• 1″ × 8″ pine
• Black and white paint

TOOLS:
• Sabre or scroll saw

DIRECTIONS:
1. Using construction paper, make and cut a pattern to the size desired or recommended. Illus. 62 and 63 can serve as guides for the pattern-making.
2. Trace the pattern onto the surface of the pine board. Make sure that the bottom of the pattern is flush with the edge of the board. By the way, you may want to make more than one loon.
3. With a sabre or scroll saw, cut out the pattern.
4. Mark the areas on the loon that should be painted black or white. Check Illus. 62 or find a picture of a loon that you can refer to. The white markings on the body, the eyes, and the lines near the bill are painted over the black paint. Allow the

Illus. 62. Loon.

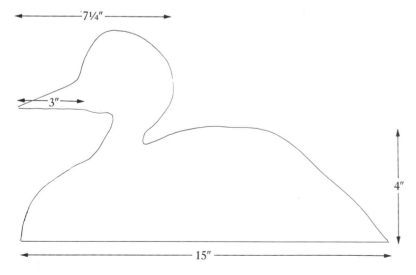

Illus. 63. Drawing of loon.

black paint to dry adequately before applying the white paint. The areas on the front and on the neck that are painted white will have black markings painted on them. Make the black markings when the white paint is dry. You need a very small brush to make the various markings. Remember, you are only approximating the appearance of a loon.

11: Desk Clock (Illus. 64

and 65)

This clock will make a very special gift for someone important to you. Best of all, it's a simple project to make. The wood can be obtained from a backyard woodpile, and the digital clock ordered from a mail-order supplier. The wood used for the clock shown in Illus. 64 is a piece of spalted red oak from a woodpile. Spalting is an effect given to wood by fungi; it's part of the decay process. When found in oak, it can be especially attractive.

MATERIAL:
• Block of firewood
• Round LCD digital clock
• Lacquer

TOOLS:
• Band or sabre saw
• Finishing sander
• Electric drill and wood bit

DIRECTIONS:
1. Find or buy an unusual chuck of wood. Many treasures can be found in the backyard woodpile or in the scrap heap at the hardwood lumber dealer. If you can find a local sawmill, explore its piles to see what you can come up with. The wood used should be distinctive looking.
2. Examine the piece of wood and decide on how it should be shaped, what surface would be the most attractive to showcase, and if the wood has to be cut in any way. You may, for example,

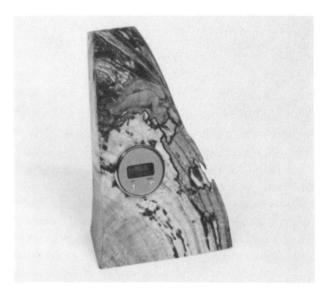

Illus. 64. Desk clock.

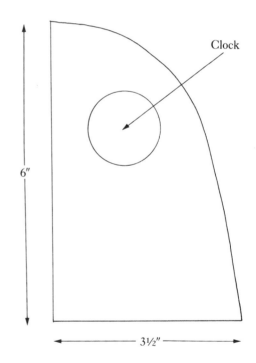

Illus. 65. Drawing of desk clock.

want to cut the base at an angle so that the clock will be easier to read.
3. Measure the back diameter of the clock that you plan to insert into the front surface of the wood. Decide where on the surface a hole should be drilled to hold the clock. If you don't have a

large enough wood bit, make the hole larger by using a small grinder with a sanding sleeve attachment. This is an effective way to enlarge a drilled hole, especially if a flange will cover up any unevenness. Drill and/or widen the hole until the clock fits snugly in place.

4. Depending upon the type of wood you used and your own personal taste, either lacquer or oil the base. You may want to glue felt dots on the bottom of the base so that it doesn't scratch the desk top.

5. Set the clock and insert it in place. Do not glue the clock in the hole, as you may have to take it out to reset it or change the battery.

12: *Display Cabinet* (Illus. 66 and 67)

If someone you know needs an open cabinet to display collectibles, this is a gift project to consider. It can be made larger or smaller than the dimensions given, depending upon need and possible placement. While the cabinet shown in Illus. 66 is made from pine, the project can also be crafted from different hardwoods. The size and number of shelves used can also be varied, depending upon need. This is an attractive, functional cabinet for any room in the house.

MATERIAL:
- 1″ × 6″ pine
- ¼″ thick battens
- Finishing nails and wire brads
- Mineral oil or lacquer
- Hangers

TOOLS:
- Sabre, band, table, or radial arm saw
- Table-mounted router and bits (rabbet and roundover bits)
- Finishing sander
- Hammer and nail set

DIRECTIONS:
1. Measure and cut the top, bottom, and side pieces to the recommended or desired dimensions. In addition to sawing the pieces to length, cut the two side pieces to their final width.

2. Using ¼″ thick battens, measure and cut sufficient amounts for two shelves, approximately 4″ and 9½″ wide, if the suggested dimensions are used. Battens are generally available at lumberyards, often in widths of 1″ or 2½″. If battens are not available from common pine, you may want to resaw shelving and backing material on the band saw.

3. With a roundover bit secured in a table-mounted router, round over the front edges of the side pieces. Note how these edges appear in Illus. 66 and 67. Do not round over the ends or the back edges of the side pieces. Round over the front and the end edges of the top and bottom pieces. Again, do not round over the back edges of these pieces.

4. Using a rabbeting bit, rout the inside back

Illus. 66. Display cabinet.

Front View   Side View

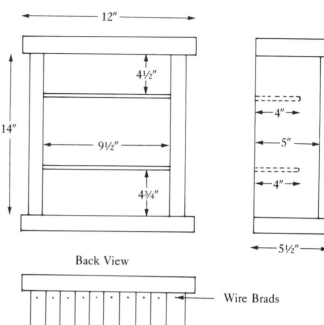

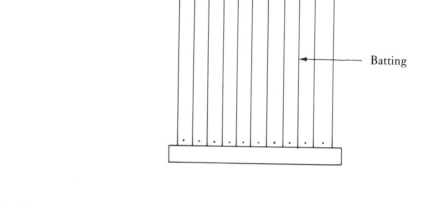

Illus. 67. Drawing of display cabinet.

Back View

Wire Brads

Batting

edges of both side pieces and the top and bottom pieces. Backing or slats will fit into these rabbeted areas. The routed area must be at least ¼″ deep. Don't try to rout this deep with one pass. Reset the bit depth and make a second pass.

5. Before assembling the cabinet, review Illus. 66 and 67. Using wood glue and finishing nails, secure the top and bottom pieces to the ends of both side pieces. All pieces should be flush in the back. Place one of the shelves inside prior to nailing, to be certain that the shelves will fit properly. The shelves should fit snugly between the side pieces. Using a nail set, drive the heads of the finishing nails under the top and bottom pieces. Wipe away any glue that may be squeezed out.

6. Measure and mark, on the inside and outside surfaces of the side pieces, exactly where the shelves are to be placed. Spread a small bead of glue on the ends of the shelves, and slip them in place. The back edge of the shelves stop at the rabbeted area. Using small finishing nails and the outer-surface line as a guide, nail the shelves in place. Drive the nail heads under the surface using the nail set. Wipe off any excess glue.

7. Measure the inside length and width of the rabbeted area on the back of the cabinet. Cut enough ¼″ thick battens to fill in this area. These batten slats should run up and down. Spread a bead of glue in the top and bottom rabbets. Set the slats in place and nail them to the rabbeted area with wire brads.

8. Using the finishing sander and fine-grit abrasive paper, prepare all surfaces for finishing. If you decide to stain the cabinet, add a clear-lacquer finish. Wipe off all dust prior to applying any finishing products.

9. Secure the shelf hangers, available at hardware stores or through mail-order suppliers, to the upper back surface of the cabinet. There are many different types of hangers available. Select a set that will best serve your needs. If you want, the cabinet can be secured to a wall with wood screws and plastic expanders. Drill small holes through the back slats for the screws to penetrate.

13: Shorebird 2 (Illus. 68 and 69)

For that person who received the first shorebird as a gift, here's a second one, with a different style. Before you're done, the recipient will be the proud owner of a covey of shorebirds. Refer to Gift Project 4 for assistance with this project.

MATERIAL:
- 3″ (12/4's) thick basswood
- ¼″ diameter dowel
- ⅛″ diameter dowel
- Slice of a fireplace log

TOOLS:
- Band saw
- Electric grinder
- Large tungsten carbide burrs
- Carving or sloyd knife
- Electric drill and bits (¼″ and ⅛″)

DIRECTIONS:
1. Draw the bird outline on the surface of the basswood or make a pattern. If basswood is not available, glue together pieces of 2″ × 6″ pine. Clamp the glued pieces.

2. Cut out the traced bud blank with a band saw with a ¼″ wide blade. Trim some of the excess wood from the blank using the band saw. Be careful.

3. Using a knife, cut the bird to its rough shape. Cut with the grain where possible. Review Illus. 68 and 69 while shaping the bird.

4. With the electric grinder and carbide burr, do the final shaping. Be certain to wear a mask and, if available, an apron. These burrs remove wood very quickly and thus generate lots of sawdust. Use the electric grinder and the burr very carefully. Read and follow the tool directions given in the manual. Clamp the bird to a board or workbench while grinding it.

5. You can also shape the bird using an electric finishing sander and coarse abrasive paper. Use 100-grit abrasive paper on the surface after you have used the grinding burr. The sander works well in shaping and finalizing the neck and head

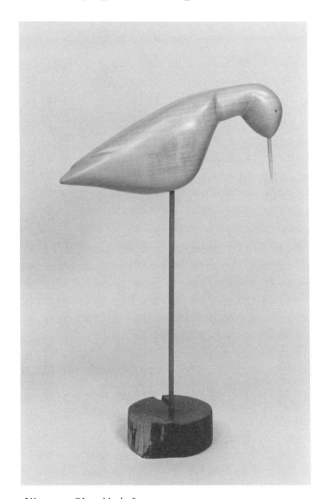

Illus. 68. Shorebird 2.

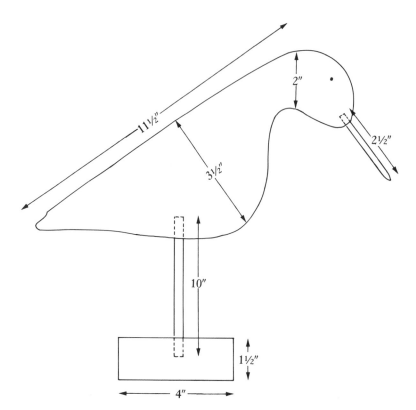

Illus. 69. Drawing of shorebird 2.

area. Use the sander to make indentations near the tail of the bird. Prepare the surface for finishing by using a series of fine-abrasive grits.

6. Approximate the location of the eyes and make small holes using either a nail or sharp punch.

7. Cut a slice from a round fireplace log for the support base.

8. In the bottom center of the bird, drill a ¼″ diameter hole approximately ¾″ deep. Note the location of the dowel in Illus. 68. Drill another hole into the support base. Cut a 10″ long piece of ¼″ diameter dowel. Insert one end into the bird, the other into the base.

9. Drill a ⅛″ diameter hole about ½″ deep where the bill should extend out from the bird's head. Measure and cut a 2½″ long piece of ⅛″ diameter dowel. Sand one end sharp, to resemble a bird's bill. Put a bit of glue on the opposite end and insert it into the drilled hole.

10. Finish the bird, base, and dowels with several coats of a clear lacquer. Using extra-fine steel wool (0000), rub the surface between coats. Wipe off the dust and wool hairs prior to applying the

next coat of lacquer. Add a final coat of paste wax and polish it with a soft rag. The result will be a project with an exceptional finish.

14: Hardwood Box (Illus. 70 and 71)

Boxes, especially hardwood boxes, are always a popular gift item. While this project is made from red oak and stained with a black walnut stain, any hardwood is acceptable for boxes. This box can be made to any size desired. It can also be crafted with a minimum of tools. If you're so inclined, add a design to the lid with a wood-burning tool, or paint on a flower or something similar.

MATERIAL:
- ⅜″ thick red oak (or other hardwood)
- Danish walnut stain
- Lacquer

Illus. 70. Hardwood box.

Side View

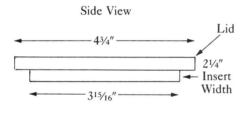

Lid

4¾″

2¼″
← Insert Width

3¹⁵⁄₁₆″

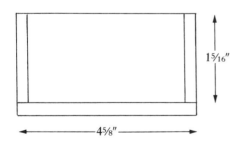

1⁵⁄₁₆″

4⁵⁄₈″

Top View

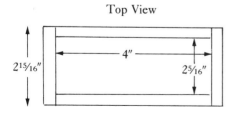

2¹⁵⁄₁₆″

4″

2⁵⁄₁₆″

Illus. 71. Drawing of hardwood box.

TOOLS:
- Band, sabre, or radial arm saw
- Finishing or belt sander

DIRECTIONS:
1. Measure and cut all pieces as presented in Illus. 71. If you are unable to obtain ⅜″ thick hardwood, resaw thicker stock using the band saw. Better yet, if you have access to a planer, plane the stock to the desired thickness. This project can also be crafted from thicker or thinner wood; just modify the dimensions accordingly. By the way, the lid and the bottom section of the box are exactly the same size.

2. Dry-assemble the box before applying glue to any surfaces. Use small rubber bands to hold it together. Check to see that all parts fit properly and are flush with one another. Check the lid insert to be certain it fits inside the box.

3. Using wood glue and rubber bands, assemble the sides and the end pieces. The rubber bands serve to clamp the joints while the glue is drying. Center and glue the insert to the inside of the lid. If available, use C-clamps on the lid and insert until the glue is dry.

4. When the glue is dry, remove the rubber bands from the box frame. Spread wood glue on the bottom edges and place on the bottom section. Secure the assembly with either rubber bands or clamps until the glue is dry.

5. Place the lid with its insert on the box and make sure that it fits. If it's too tight, remove some edge surface from the insert using a sander.

6. Using either a belt or finishing sander, prepare all surfaces for finishing. If you plan to wood-burn a design on the lid, now is the time to do it. You may want to lightly pencil the design on the lid and then burn it in with the unit.

7. If you decide to stain the box, carefully read the label directions on the can. As a rule, the longer the stain remains on the wood's surface, the darker it will become. Practise on a scrap piece of the same kind of wood that the project is made from. When the stain is completely dry, add a clear-lacquer finish to the box.

15: *Garden Box* (Illus. 72 and 73)

This Early American box is a perfect container for garden tools. It can also serve as a magazine holder or simply as a decorative box for placement in a room or near the fireplace. It is made from pine and painted, and can be made larger or smaller than shown in Illus. 72 and 73, depending upon need.

MATERIAL:
- ½″ thick pine
- Finishing nails
- Paint

TOOLS:
- Sabre saw
- Finishing sander
- Electric drill and bit (⅜″)
- Table-mounted router and roundover bit

DIRECTIONS:
1. Purchase or plane common pine to a ½″ thickness. Measure and cut all pieces for the box.
2. Draw a finger-grip area on the center board. Review Illus. 72 or 73 before doing this. Drill a hole through the drawn area. This will allow you to insert a blade from a sabre saw to cut out the area.

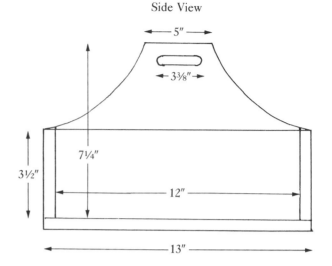

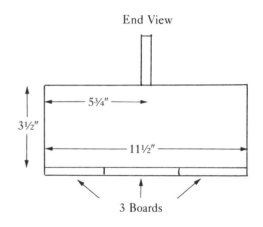

Illus. 72. Drawing of garden box.

Illus. 73. Garden box.

3. Using a roundover bit, rout the edges of the boards. Also rout the finger-grip area.

4. Assemble the box using wood glue and finishing nails. Use a nail set to tap the nail heads under the surface of the wood. Wipe off any excess glue.

5. Sand and prepare the surfaces for finishing. As indicated, you may want to consider painting this project.

16: *Framed Sculpted Inlay* (Illus. 74 and 75)

This very decorative piece gives you the opportunity to exploit some attractive woods and your own artistic tendencies. The inlay is a free-form shaped from a scrap piece of bocote, an imported hardwood. It is set in a backing of black walnut and supported, in the frame, by a piece of inexpensive plywood. The frame, with mitred joints, is an attractive piece of hard maple. It is the exact frame, but different wood, that was presented in Project 2.

Illus. 74. Framed sculpted inlay.

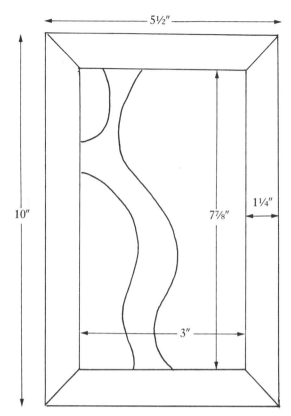

Illus. 75. Drawing of framed sculpted inlay.

MATERIAL:

- 1″ (4/4's) thick hardwood for the frame
- ¼″ thick hardwood for the backing
- 1″ (4/4's) thick hardwood for the inlay
- ⅛″ thick plywood
- Mineral oil or lacquer

TOOLS:

- Band or table saw
- Sabre saw
- Mitre saw
- Table-mounted router and bits (roundover and rabbeting)
- Moto or flex-shaft tool with sanding sleeves
- Finishing sander

DIRECTIONS:

1. Refer to Gift Project 2 for directions on making the frame. After the frame is completed, the inlay tasks can be started.

2. Measure and cut the ⅛″ thick plywood piece

that will fit inside the back, rabbeted area of the frame.

3. Measure and cut the ¼″ thick piece of hardwood that will serve as the backing for the inlay. The wood should contrast or set off the inlay. The backing fits inside the frame, on top of the plywood, so check the measurements.

4. Find a piece of scrap wood for the actual inlay. Draw a design and cut it out. Using a moto or flex-shaft tool and abrasive sleeves, shape the inlay. Leave the back edges sharp. Refer to Illus. 74 for ideas on shaping.

5. Decide where the inlay is to be placed on the piece of backing, and trace it onto its surface. Cut out, on the outside of the line, the traced inlay design.

6. Place the plywood into the rabbeted areas and then place the backing pieces and the inlay inside the frame. You may have to sand some edge from the backing pieces to get a good fit.

7. Using wood glue, secure the plywood piece into the frame. Allow it to dry. Spread wood glue on the front surface of the plywood and set the backing pieces and the inlay in place. Wipe off any excess glue. Allow the assembly to dry.

8. Finish the project using either a clear lacquer or oil.

9. Cut out and glue a piece of construction paper over the back of the frame. Measure and place a hanger on the back. You may want to drill an angled hole into the back, to use for hanging the project.

17: *Diddle Sticks* (Illus. 76 and 77)

These fun devices will make an ideal gift for those executives who need something to tap or chew on, to dissipate nervous energy. Best of all, the sticks can be turned from scraps of hardwood. To protect the user, finish them with mineral oil, a non-toxic finish.

MATERIAL:
• 1″ (4/4's) thick hardwood
• Mineral oil

TOOLS:
• Wood lathe
• Prong center and ball-bearing center
• Spindle gouge

Illus. 76. Diddle sticks.

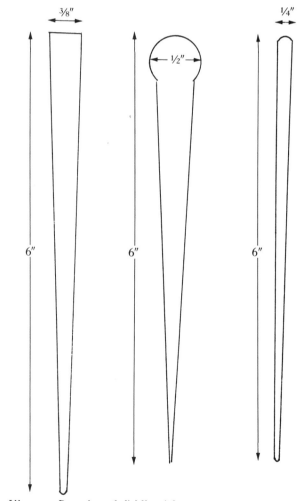

Illus. 77. Drawing of diddle sticks.

48

DIRECTIONS:

1. Cut hardwood blanks into a variety of lengths and thicknesses. Use scrap pieces of hardwood. An average finished diddle stick is approximately 6″ long.

2. Secure the blanks between centers and turn. This project provides an excellent opportunity to refine or develop your turning skills. If you have one of the commercial chucks for your lathe, use it for turning the sticks. Use the skew to taper some of the sticks. You will find that small projects like the diddle stick are great fun to turn.

3. Add a mineral oil or lacquer finish to the sticks, depending on your preference.

18: Desk Scratch-Paper Holder (Illus. 78 and 79)

The project was designed and crafted by Andy Matoesian for his desk. Made with black walnut and enhanced with a routed and sawed top surface, the holder is an excellent focal-point piece on any desk. You may prefer using a choice piece of hardwood on the top of the holder rather than the detailed surface. As with most of the projects, the dimensions can also be modified to meet specific needs. The scratch paper can be cut to size.

MATERIAL:

- ¾″ (3/4's) thick hardwood
- Scratch paper
- Lacquer or mineral oil

TOOLS:

- Band, radial arm, or sabre saw
- Table-mounted router and bits (cove and straight)
- Finishing sander
- Clamps

DIRECTIONS:

1. Measure and saw the components using Illus. 78 and 79 as guides. As indicated, you may want to modify the design or dimensions based on specific needs or available material.

2. The curved open area on the front piece should be laid out and cut. Use a sabre saw or a band saw with a narrow blade.

3. Depending upon your design preference, you may want to enhance the top piece with various router cuts or leave it plain.

4. Using wood glue and clamps, assemble the holder and allow the glue to dry. (Rubber bands can also be used for clamps. They are not as effective, but they will work.) Wipe any excess glue from the surfaces.

5. Finish the holder with either lacquer or oil.

6. Cut scrap paper to fit the internal dimensions of the holder.

Illus. 78. Desk scratch-paper holder.

Top View

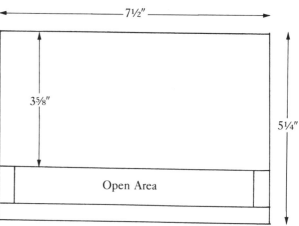

7½"

3⅝"

5¼"

Open Area

Illus. 79. Drawing of desk scratch-paper holder.

Front View

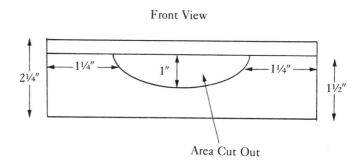

2¼"

1¼"

1"

1¼"

1½"

Area Cut Out

19: *Americana Lath Design* (Illus. 80 and 81)

If you're inclined to making a gift that's a bit different, yet one that projects a sense of Americana, lath designs may be for you. Lath art for hanging pieces is always popular and easy to do. If you are unable to obtain lath from the local lumber dealer, cut strips from pine boards. While this project presents a flag-type design, you may prefer something totally different. Using pencil and paper, design a project made from laths and then craft and paint it. As you may be aware, lath pieces appear two-dimensional.

MATERIAL:
- ¼" thick plywood
- Lath or ¼" thick pine strips
- Wire brads
- Wood glue
- Paint

TOOLS:
- Band saw
- Sabre or scroll saw

DIRECTIONS:
1. Design your project, with dimensions, on paper. Some of the lath in lath art is elevated from the surface. This creates a two-dimensional appearance.

Illus. 80. *Americana lath design.*

Illus. 81. *Drawing of Americana lath design.*

Heart

9″

2⅝″

3⅝″

4¾″

⅜″ Wide Strips
¼″ Thick

7 Red Stripes
6 White Stripes
(Background)

Side View

1″

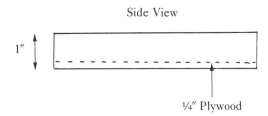

¼″ Plywood

2. If lath is not available, cut lath from pine boards using a band saw and fence. Make the lath uniform both in width and thickness.

3. Depending upon the size of your project, cut a piece of ¼" thick plywood for backing. When assembled, the plywood should be inside the frame of lath that surrounds the design. The lath will be glued and nailed to the plywood.

4. Without gluing or nailing any parts, lay out the lath design on the plywood backing. Check the design and the various dimensions. Make any corrections.

5. Paint each of the component parts their appropriate color. For example, on the project design the seven stripes are painted red. The portion of plywood under the stripe area is painted white. The heart is painted red, and the areas that are under it and frame it are painted blue. The frame is left unpainted. Do all painting before assembling the project.

6. Using glue and wire brads, assemble the lath into the planned design on the plywood backing. Glue and nail the lath frame around it.

7. Center and nail a sawtooth hanger on the back for hanging the project.

20: *Round Cutting Board* (Illus. 82 and 83)

A round cutting board is a project that makes sense for both the recipient and the giver. Its size and shape make it ideal for regular countertop use. Its round shape makes it relatively easy to make. The wood used for this project was a scrap piece of sycamore. While not as solid as hard rock maple, it is a good wood to use when you want to maximize your scraps.

MATERIAL:
• 1" (4/4's) thick hardwood
• Mineral oil

TOOLS:
• Band or sabre saw
• School compass
• Table-mounted router and roundover bit
• Drill press
• 1¼" diameter multi-spur bit
• Finishing sander

Illus. 82. Round cutting board.

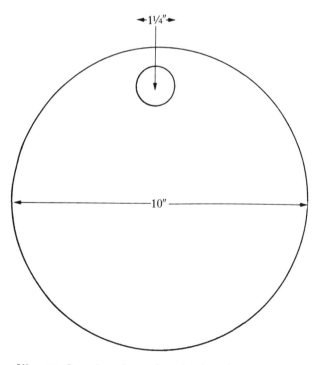

Illus. 83. Drawing of round cutting board.

DIRECTIONS:

1. Set and use a school compass to draw a circle on the wood's surface. The circle's diameter may be modified, based on available material.

2. Carefully, to maintain its roundness, cut out the board using either a band or sabre saw.

3. If a hanging/finger-grip hole is desired, use a drill press and a multi-spur bit, if they are available, to drill a hole through the board as indicated in Illus. 83. A smaller hole can be drilled, if desired, with an electric drill and a wood bit.

4. Set the roundover bit to an appropriate depth and rout both edges of the cutting board. If drilled, also rout the hanging/finger hole.

5. Using a series of fine-abrasive grits, prepare all surfaces for finishing.

6. Finish the cutting board with mineral oil.

Illus. 84. Children's book holder.

21: Children's Book Holder (Illus. 84 and 85)

Always a popular and useful gift item for people of all ages, book holders are easy and fun to make. Once you understand how to make a holder, you can make almost any design. The one featured here has a cat design. Book holders present you with lots of possibilities not only for crafting, but also for painting or decorating.

MATERIAL:
- 1″ × 8″ pine
- ⅝″ diameter dowels
- Clear, green marbles
- Black paint

TOOLS:
- Sabre or scroll saw
- Electric drill and bit (⅝″)
- Countersink or electric drill

DIRECTIONS:

1. Using construction paper and Illus. 85, make and cut a full-size pattern of the cat. If you plan on using a different design, make a pattern of it.

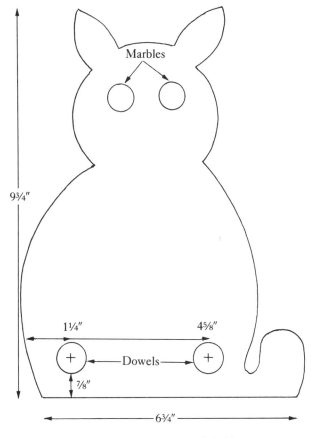

Illus. 85. Drawing of children's book holder.

Patterns are very helpful in crafting. They not only help you to duplicate the same design, but they can be saved for future use. Trace the pattern on the board's surface, with the grain. You have to make two cats, one for each end of the holder.

2. Saw the traced cats or designs from the board.

3. Measure and mark the location of the two dowel holes and the eyes on both front surfaces.

4. If ⅝″ diameter dowels are to be used, drill the dowel holes with a ⅝″ diameter bit. Move the bit through the holes several times in order to slightly widen them. The dowels should slide freely in the holes.

5. Use either a large twist drill or countersink to make indentations for the eyes. When it's time to secure the eyes to the cat, spread glue in the small indentations and set the marbles in place until the glue is dry.

6. Measure and cut to length two pieces of ⅝″ diameter dowel. The length of the dowels should be determined by possible placement of the book holder and the number of books you want it to hold. Make sure that the dowels slide freely through the drilled holes. If not, enlarge the holes using a round rasp or by moving the bit in and out of the hole.

7. Paint the cat and the dowels.

8. When the paint is dry, spread white glue in the eye indentations and set the marbles in place. Allow the cats to remain flat while the glue dries.

9. Slide the dowels in place and adjust them for use.

22: *Pipe Tools* (Illus. 86 and 87)

Pipe tools turned from one of the exotic woods, and small enough for regular use, will endear you to the pipe smoker. These scrapers and tappers are standard items designed for pipes. They are made of aluminum and easy to cut into two sections for integration into the turned pieces. To make the holder more durable, small brass rings are cut and slipped over the bottom tenon of the tool. If you're a wood turner, you'll have lots of fun with this project.

MATERIAL:

- 1″ (4/4's) thick hardwood
- Pipe tool
- Brass tubing (½″ diameter)
- Mineral oil or lacquer

TOOLS:

- Wood lath and turning tools
- Hacksaw
- Electric drill and bit (³⁄₁₆″)

DIRECTIONS:

1. Measure and cut a series of square turning blanks from approximately 1″ (4/4's) thick stock. While exotic woods are ideal for this project, any hardwood will do. You may want to look in the scrap box for some pieces with interesting grain or color. The blanks can be from 3″ to 5″ long.

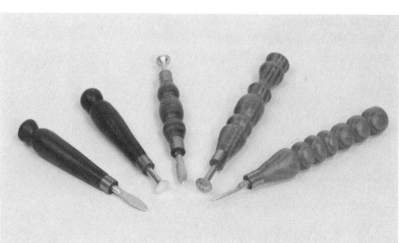

Illus. 86. Pipe tools.

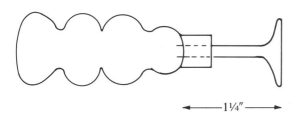

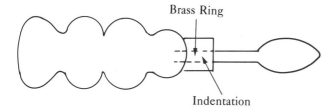

Illus. 87. *Drawing of pipe tools.*

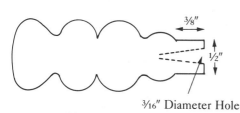

The longer tools can be used on top of the desk, while the smaller devices can be carried in a pocket.

2. Mount the blanks between the centers or in a chuck and turn them. Note the dimensions for the bottom tenon on the tool shown in Illus. 87. The tenon needs to be turned to accommodate a piece of brass tubing. It should have a slight taper to better hold the brass ring in place. Use a vernier caliper to check your measurements.

3. Using a hacksaw, cut the aluminum pipe tool into two sections. Check the diameter of the aluminum shaft. With abrasive paper, slightly taper the end portion that will penetrate the tool handle.

4. Drill a ³⁄₁₆″ diameter hole or whatever diameter the pipe tool shaft happens to be in the handle tenon. Penetrate at least ½″ with the bit. Make sure that you drill the hole straight.

5. Measure the length of the handle tenon and, using the hacksaw, cut a brass ring to length. Slip

the ring over the tenon and tap it in place. If it's a bit long, sand it flush while it is in place.

6. Place the aluminum shaft into the tenon hole and tap it into the tenon. Don't hit the shaft too hard or it will bend. Take your time with this task. If the shaft should bend, straighten it out with pliers and continue tapping it until it is in place. Check Illus. 86.

7. Using a hammer and nail, tap several indentations in the ring at various locations, to ensure that the brass ring does not slip off.

8. Finish the project with lacquer or oil.

23: *Key Holder 1* (Illus. 88 and 89)

Key holders are always popular gift items. While you can make them in any design, the large key shape used for this project is especially appropri-

Illus. 88. Key holder 1.

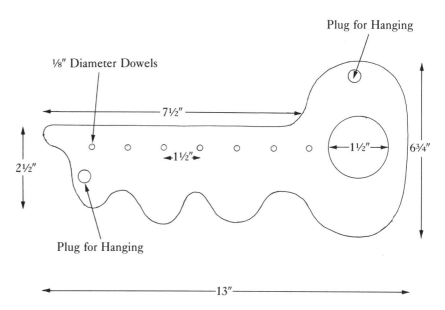

Illus. 89. Drawing of key holder 1.

ate. This key holder was crafted and designed by Wendell Meyer. The project allows you the opportunity to try tole-painting or other type of decoration.

MATERIAL:
- 1″ × 8″ pine
- ⅛″ diameter dowels
- ½″ diameter plugs
- Paint

TOOLS:
- Sabre or scroll saw
- Table-mounted router and beading bit
- Electric drill and bits (⅛″, ½″, and 1½″)
- Finishing sander

DIRECTIONS:
1. While the project can be drawn freehand onto the surface of the board, a pattern always works best. Make a pattern from construction paper and

trace it onto the board. Cut out the traced project.

2. Measure and mark the location for the large hole in the key handle. Using a 1½″ diameter spade bit or a drill press and hole cutter, make the large hole in the handle.

3. Check the suggested dimensions shown in Illus. 89 and measure and mark the location of the dowels. While seven dowels are used for this project, you may want to increase the number in order to accommodate more keys. If ⅛″ diameter dowels are to be used, drill ⅛″ diameter holes where marked. Drill them all to the same depth.

4. Locate where the two hanging holes should be placed and drill ½″ diameter holes to accommodate both a screw and a plug. Refer to Illus. 89. The holes should be at least ⅜″ deep.

5. Rout the front edges and the handle hole. Do not rout the back edges.

6. Prepare the surfaces for finishing.

7. Measure and cut ⅛″ diameter dowels to a length of 1½″. Place a spot of glue on the ends of the dowels and tap them into their holes. They should all extend the same distance from the surface. Sand the rough edge on the top of each dowel. Wipe away any excess glue.

8. Paint and decorate as desired. Be sure to paint the plugs that will cover the heads of the hanging screws.

24: *Covey of Quail* (Illus. 90 and 91)

While you can make just one, quail should be in a covey. A hen and several chicks, shaped from chunks of hardwood, make a gift that someone will love. As with the shorebirds, these quail are approximations of the real things. You do not have to be a master carver to make this project. A few basic tools, blocks of wood, and a touch of imagination are all that are needed. The quail shown in Illus. 90 were made from chunks of black walnut that were found in a woodpile. Any kind of hardwood is acceptable.

MATERIAL:
- 4″ (16/4's) thick hardwood
- 1 ¾″ (7/4's) thick hardwood
- Lacquer

TOOLS:
- Band saw
- Electric grinder and carbide burr
- Finishing sander
- Carving or sloyd knife

DIRECTIONS:
1. Look for dry logs or chunks of wood from the woodpile that you can use. If none are available, find chunks of low-grade walnut or similar hardwood at your dealer. Basewood is acceptable, but you can also use a different hardwood. Prepare the wood into carving blocks and draw the quail on the surfaces.

2. Using a band saw with a ¼″ wide blade, cut out the shapes. Remove some of the excess wood with the band saw. Do this task carefully.

3. Shape the hen and chicks using the various tools available to you. Refer to Gift Project 4 for some ideas. Be careful with these tools, and wear a face guard. Use Illus. 90 as a guide.

Illus. 90. Covey of quail.

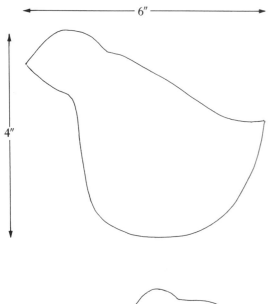

6″

4″

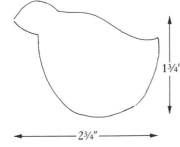

1¾″

2¾″

Illus. 91. Drawing of quail.

MATERIAL:
- ½″ thick pine
- Sheet metal
- 1″ diameter dowel
- Buckskin lace
- Nails and screw
- Grey paint

TOOLS:
- Band or sabre saw
- Electric drill and bit (¼″)
- Screwdriver
- Finishing sander
- Tin snips

DIRECTIONS:
1. Using Illus. 93 as a guide, measure and cut out the various parts. The ends of the back piece where the dowel will be attached must be cut at an approximate 15-degree angle. This makes the taper of the dustpan possible. You may have to experiment with different angles to get the dust-

4. When shaped and carved to your satisfaction, go over the surface of each piece with a series of abrasive grits on the finishing sander. Final shaping can be done with this process, if desired. Prepare surfaces for finishing.

5. A clear lacquer, rubbed between coats with steel wool, makes an attractive finish for the hen and chicks.

25: *Dustpan* (Illus. 92 and 93)

This is a practical gift that, if made properly, will become the dustpan of choice in the recipient's house. In that the design is Early American and the dustpan looks like a collectible, it may be displayed in a prominent place. You may want to stencil or do decorative painting on part of the dustpan.

Illus. 92. Dustpan.

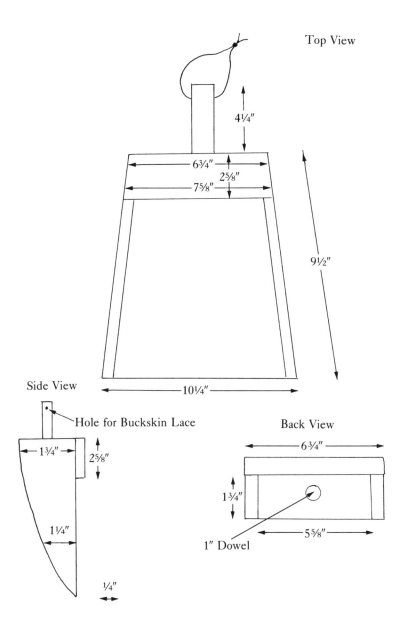

Top View

4¼"

6¾"

2⅝"

7⅝"

9½"

10¼"

Side View

Hole for Buckskin Lace

1¾"

2⅝"

1¼"

¼"

Illus. 93. Drawing of dustpan.

Back View

6¾"

1¾"

5⅝"

1" Dowel

pan at the correct taper. The angle cuts can be made with a sabre or band saw. If you don't have ½" thick pine, resaw enough for the project using a band saw with a ½" wide blade. Sand the rough surfaces with a belt sander.

2. Assemble the various cut pieces using wood glue and finishing nails. Measure and mark the center of the back for placement of the dowel. Cut a 4½" long piece of 1" diameter dowel. Using wood glue and a wood screw, secure the dowel handle in place. Refer to Illus. 93 for assistance.

3. Place the assembled dustpan frame on the surface of the sheet metal. The edge of the metal can serve as the front edge of the dustpan. Using an alcohol pen, trace all the outer edges of the frame onto the metal's surface. With tin snips or another cutter, cut the sheet metal along the traced lines. Be careful; don't cut yourself on the sharp edges.

4. Starting at the back, using small nails with heads, nail the sheet metal to the bottom edges of the frame. You may have to use extra nails near the front of the pan. Be careful not to split the frame with the nails.

5. Sand lightly all the edges and surfaces using a finishing sander. Remove any burrs from the metal using the sander.

6. Drill a ¼″ diameter hole through the dowel handle. After the dustpan is painted, thread and tie a piece of buckskin lace through the hole for hanging.

7. Paint the project as desired.

26: *Fireplace Tools* (Illus. 94 and 95)

A fine set of turned fireplace tools can be made with large railroad tie nails and a few pieces of hardwood. While this project was made from black walnut, you may prefer a different hardwood. Try to use scraps.

MATERIAL:
- 2″ (8/4's) thick hardwood
- Railroad tie nails
- 1″ diameter copper rings
- Buckskin lace
- Lacquer

TOOLS:
- Wood lathe and turning tools
- Propane torch
- Electric drill and bit (¼″ and ⅜″)
- File
- Hacksaw

DIRECTIONS:
1. Prepare turning blanks that are at least 13″ long and 2″ (8/4's) thick. Mount them on the lathe between the prong drive and revolving center and turn. Using Illus. 94 and 95 as guides, turn both handles. Note the tenon that must be turned on each handle. Give it a slight taper at the front so that the copper ring will fit over it easily. Use a vernier caliper to measure the inside diameter of the copper ring and then transfer it to the tenon diameter.

2. Using a hacksaw, cut the nail head off each nail. With a file, round over the edge and give it a slight taper. This end will be placed into the tool handle.

3. One of the nails has to be bent approximately 1½″ from its end. While you can try bending the nail with a hammer, you may have more success by heating it with a torch and then bending it. The bend in the nail allows the user to more easily pull and roll a burning log.

4. Drill a ⅜″ diameter hole into the tenon of each handle. The holes should be at least an 1¼″ deep.

5. Slip the copper rings over the tenons and tap

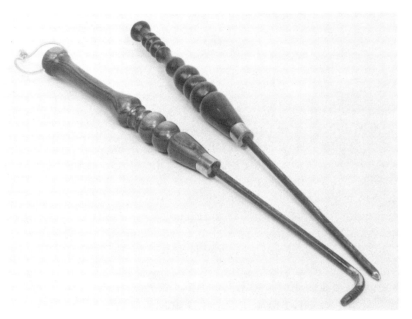

Illus. 94. Fireplace tools.

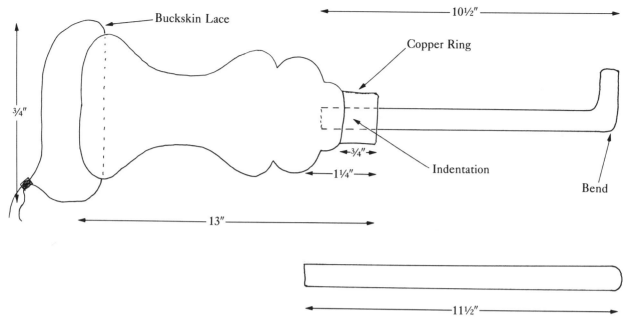

Buckskin Lace

Copper Ring

10½"

¾"

¾"

1¼"

Indentation

Bend

13"

11½"

Illus. 95. Drawing of fireplace tools.

them in place. Use a file, if necessary, to make the tenons and rings flush.

6. Squirt some wood glue in the tenon holes and tap the nails in place. Drive them all the way to the bottom of the drilled holes.

7. With a nail, make several indentations into the surface of the copper rings. This prevents them from slipping off during use.

8. Drill a ¼" diameter hole in the upper section of each handle. After the handles have been finished, thread a piece of buckskin through the holes and tie it, to use for hanging.

9. Finish the handles using a clear lacquer or a finish of choice.

27: Sewing Caddie (Illus. 96 and 97)

This caddie is a useful device for any household, and especially for those small sewing jobs. It can be left on a shelf or in a convenient spot for all members of the family to use. It is made from a piece of walnut and has a bright-red-and-green pin cushion attached to it.

MATERIAL:
- ⅝" thick hardwood
- ⅛" diameter dowels
- Pin cushion
- Finishing nail

TOOLS:
- Wood lathe
- Band or sabre saw
- Electric drill and bit (⅛")
- Electric finishing sander
- Table-mounted router and roundover bit

Illus. 96. Sewing caddie.

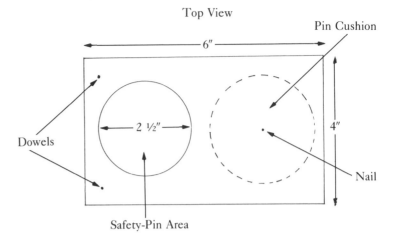

Illus. 97. Drawing of sewing caddie.

Top View

Pin Cushion

6"

Dowels

2 ½"

4"

Nail

Safety-Pin Area

DIRECTIONS:

1. Glue a pine block to the back of the hardwood piece that has been cut to the suggested dimensions. Any species of hardwood with a thickness of at least ½" will work. The block should be placed below the area that will be turned as a pin holder. Attach a faceplate, secure the block to the lathe, and turn the pin area. A small round-nose scraper works well for this task. Remove the glue block and clean up the base with a sander.
2. Rout all the edges. Sand all the surfaces with fine-grit abrasives.
3. Drill ⅛" diameter holes in the surface to hold the thread dowels. Cut two ⅛" diameter pieces of dowel 1¾" long, spread glue on one end, and place it in the drilled holes.
4. In the area where the pin cushion is to be placed, locate its center. Drive a 1" finishing nail or one about that size into the marked center. Sand or file the head of the nail to a point. It should be able to penetrate the fabric on the pine cushion.
5. Finish the sewing caddie with a clear lacquer.
6. Spread white glue on the surface around the cushion nail and force the pin cushion in place. Allow the glue to dry.

28: Barnyard Chickens

(Illus. 98 and 99)

This is a fun project to make and, once you get started, you will want to craft flocks of chickens.

Both roosters and a hen can be easily made and painted by the amateur. Best of all, each can be made so that it is different in size and design. All can stand in different poses.

MATERIAL:
- 1" × 8" pine
- ¼" dowels
- Fireplace logs
- Black, yellow, red, and white paint

TOOLS:
- Band, sabre, or scroll saw
- Electric drill and bit (¼")
- Finishing sander

DIRECTIONS:

1. Draw and cut patterns for the chickens from construction paper. Review Illus. 98 and 99 for guidelines and approximate dimensions.
2. Trace the patterns onto the surface of 1" × 8" pine boards and cut them out using either a sabre or scroll saw. Give the roosters sharp tail-feather detail as you cut them.
3. If you can find a 3" to 4" diameter round log on the woodpile, slice it into two sections. Cut chunks that are about 5" to 6" long for the support bases for the chickens.
4. Depending upon how you want the chickens to appear, drill the ¼" diameter dowel holes accordingly. They should be at least ½" deep both in the chicken and in the center of the support base.

Illus. 98. *Barnyard chickens.*

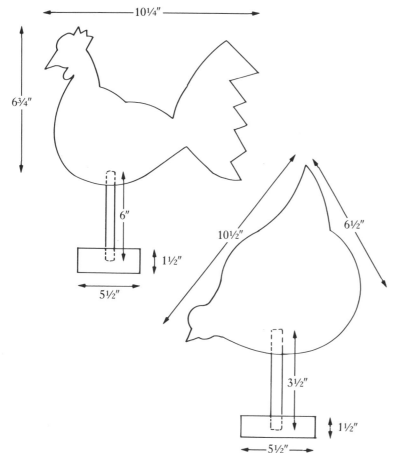

Illus. 99. *Drawing of barnyard chickens.*

5. Cut ¼″ diameter dowels to the desired length and insert them in place.

6. Using the finishing sander, go over all surfaces both on the chickens and the support bases, preparing them for painting. Wipe off all dust.

7. Paint the chickens as desired.

29: Musical-Note Compact-Disc Holder

(Illus. 100 and 101)

This clever, accessible device for holding compact discs will make a welcomed gift. The design of the holder makes the back edge of each disc visible and easy to read. While a musical note is not original, any design can be used for holder ends. Once you understand how the holder is made, you can develop your own unique designs. Also, you may want to significantly increase the size of the holder. This can be done by simply using longer dowels.

MATERIAL:
- 1″ × 8″ pine
- ¾″ diameter dowels
- Black paint

TOOLS:
- Sabre or scroll saw
- Electric drill and wood bit (¾″)
- Table-mounted router and roundover bit
- Finishing sander

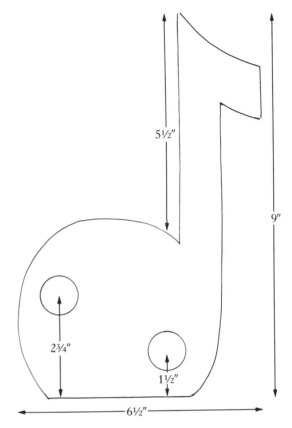

Illus. 101. Drawing of musical-note compact-disc holder.

DIRECTIONS:

1. As always, make a pattern to size using construction paper. Check the various dimensions of the holder as presented in Illus. 101. The notes can be made larger than suggested. Trace the pattern, with the grain, onto the surface of a 1″ × 8″ pine board.

2. Cut the traced notes from the pine board using either a sabre or scroll saw.

3. Rout all edges, except the bottom of each note, using a roundover bit. Use a piece of scrap to check the depth of cut of the bit before routing the notes.

4. Measure, mark, and drill the ¾″ diameter holes through both notes. Widen the drilled holes by passing and moving the bit through the holes several times. The dowels have to move freely through the holes. Cut two pieces of dowel to length. Check the dowels and the holes for fit. If too tight, widen them further.

5. Prepare all surfaces using the finishing sander

Illus. 100. Musical-note compact-disc holder.

and fine-grit abrasive papers. Remove all dust.
6. Paint the note and dowels black or any color of choice. Avoid getting any paint in the dowel holes. Allow the note and dowels to dry.

30: Potato Masher/Mallet

(Illus. 102 and 103)

While a functional device for the kitchen or the shop, mashers and mallets as part of Americana are often collected and displayed. When turned from oak, walnut, osage orange, or some other indigenous wood, they are especially prized. Search for dry logs on the woodpile than you can use, or for scraps, if available.

Don't forget to make some mallets for yourself to use in the shop. They're very useful when you need to tap a carving tool or something else where a hammer won't do the job.

MATERIAL:
- 4" (16/4's) thick hardwood
- Mineral oil

TOOLS:
- Wood lathe and turning tools
- Band saw

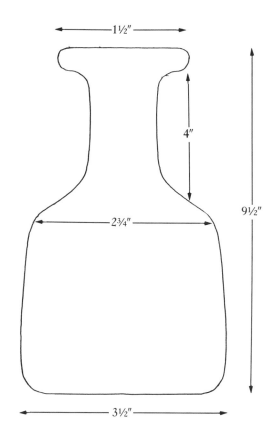

Illus. 103. Drawing of potato masher/mallet.

Illus. 102. Potato masher/mallet.

DIRECTIONS:
1. Measure and cut the turning blanks to length. Make the project any size that you want and from any wood that's available. As indicated, dry chunks from the woodpile are an excellent source for wood of this thickness. Smaller-diameter stock can also be used.
2. Secure the blank on the lathe between a four-prong center and a revolving-cone center. If you're a spindle turner, this can be done quickly and easily. For those who are not familiar with the lathe, turn the entire project using a 1" round-nose scraper. See Illus. 102 and 103 to determine the shape and the approximate dimensions.
3. If needed, sand the project while it is between centers.
4. Put an oil finish on the mallets and mashers.

31: Child's Stool/Chair

(Illus. 104 and 105)

This practical gift has a universal design in which the back rest folds down to become the step for the stool. Toddlers, parents, and grandparents will all find uses for this gift. There is a lot of surface on this stool to paint names, animals, or bright decorations, if you're so inclined.

MATERIAL:
- 1" × 8" pine
- 1" × 4" pine
- ½" diameter dowels
- 1" diameter wooden wheels
- Wood screws and plugs
- Finishing nails
- Paint

TOOLS:
- Sabre, band, radial arm, or table saw
- Table-mounted router and roundover bit
- Electric drill and bits (¹⁄₁₆" and ½")
- Finishing sander

DIRECTIONS:
1. Carefully study Illus. 104 and 105. While the project may seem initially very difficult, it is not. There are, however, several different parts to measure, cut, and assemble.

2. Using the 1" × 8" stock, measure and cut the two legs and the seat. Measure and mark the location of the two dowels on the sides of the legs and drill the holes. If you are using ½" diameter dowels, use a ½" diameter drill bit. Measure and mark the location of the moveable arms on the outside surface of each leg. Refer to Illus. 105 for dimensions.

3. Rout the edges of the legs and the seat. Do not rout edges that join other edges, for example, the bottom, end edges of the seat section.

4. Using wood glue, nails, or wood screws and ½" diameter plugs, assemble the seat to the legs. Cut two ½" diameter dowels to length and place them through the holes in the leg. Glue them in

place. Make sure that the dowels extend out from the outside surface of the legs. See Illus. 105.

5. Design, measure, and cut one moveable arm. Refer to Illus. 105 for guidance concerning the shape and dimensions. Trace the second arm from the first. Measure and mark the screw hole on the bottom, outer surface of each arm. Using a ½" diameter bit, drill a hole at the marks approximately ¼" deep. This area will accommodate the head of the wood screw as the project is assembled. At the center of each ½" hole, drill a ¹⁄₁₆" diameter hole through the arm. This hole will prevent the wood from cracking when the wood screw penetrates, but also will allow free movement of the arm. Rout all edges except where the step piece will be attached.

6. Measure and cut the step piece that attaches to the two arms. Rout the edges.

7. Using a wood screw that is approximately 1¼" long, thread it through the drilled holes in the arm and through the hole in the 1" diameter wooden wheel, and screw it into the outside of the leg where marked. Repeat the process with the other arm.

8. Attach the step piece to the arms using wood glue, nails, or wood screws and plugs.

9. Paint and decorate the stool.

Illus. 104. Child's stool/chair.

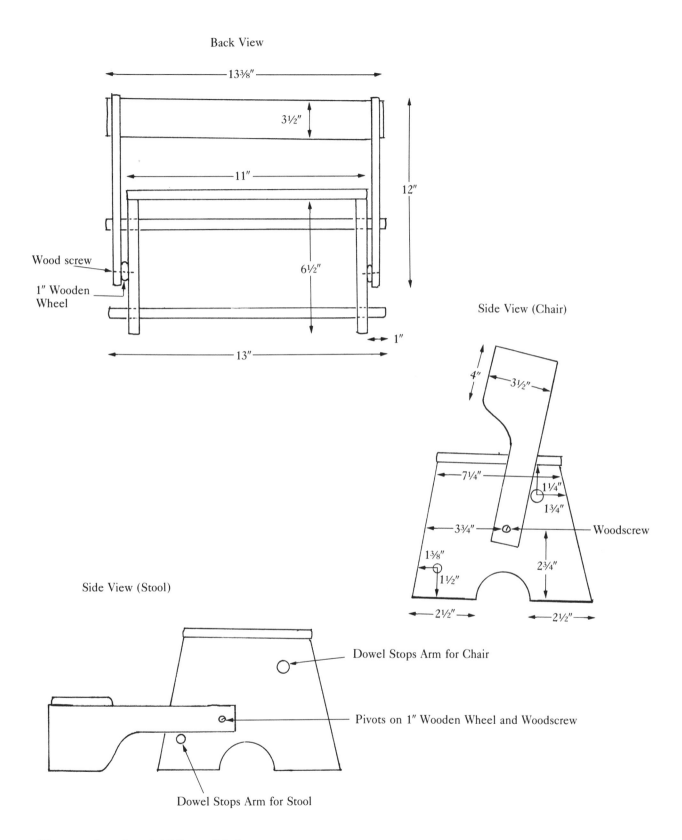

Back View

13⅜″

3½″

11″

12″

Wood screw

1″ Wooden Wheel

6½″

1″

13″

Side View (Chair)

4″

3½″

7¼″

1¼″

1¾″

3¾″

Woodscrew

1⅜″

2¾″

1½″

2½″

2½″

Side View (Stool)

Dowel Stops Arm for Chair

Pivots on 1″ Wooden Wheel and Woodscrew

Dowel Stops Arm for Stool

Illus. 105. Drawing of child's stool/chair.

32: *Earrings* (Illus. 106 and 107)

For those who enjoy earrings of a different style and made from exotic woods, this will prove to be an ideal gift. Using only scraps of such exotic woods as bocote, padauk, and ebony, you can make lots of earrings. Avoid using any of the imports that are considered toxic or could cause skin reactions. Usually your wood dealer can point these species out for you. And don't rule out using indigenous woods such as walnut, osage orange, and cherry. The various metal components and veneer are available from mail-order suppliers.

MATERIAL:

- Scrap hardwoods (imports and indigenous)
- Veneer
- Super Glue
- Earring posts, wires, clips, and rings
- Double-face tape
- Oil and lacquer

TOOLS:

- Band, scroll, or sabre saw
- Drill press and bit (1/16″)
- 1/2″ diameter plug cutter
- Finishing sander
- Belt sander
- Clamps

DIRECTIONS:

1. To make the round earrings presented in Illus. 107, use a 1/2″ diameter plug cutter and a drill press. With the hardwood of choice, cut several plugs.

2. Set the band-saw fence to cut slices from the plug that are approximately 1/8″ thick.

3. Place strips of double-face tape on a small piece of scrap. Then place the slices on the tape. Align the grain so that the surfaces are sanded and not scratched. Sand the slices on both sides.

4. Using Super Glue, secure the earring post near the top edge of the back surface of a slice. Carefully follow the directions on the glue label. Repeat the process until the posts have been secured to all slices. Finish the earrings with oil or lacquer.

5. Cut design 2 in Illus. 107 from 1/8″ thick material. Make a pattern for a design and trace it onto the surface of the hardwood. Cut the traced design using a scroll or sabre saw. Sand the surfaces and finish them with either oil or lacquer. Drill 1/16″ diameter holes near the top edge to accommodate a metal ring. Attach the earring wire to the ring.

6. Cut designs 3 and 4 from two pieces of scrap with a piece of red veneer glued between them. To make the veneered stock, spread wood glue on the surfaces and clamp them until the glue is dried. Using a band saw, cut slices of veneered

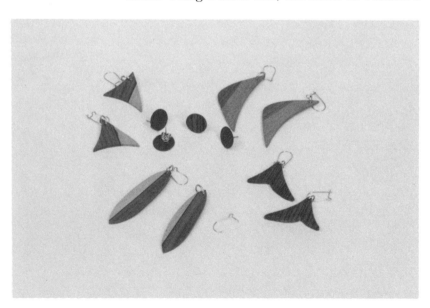

Illus. 106. Earrings.

Design 1

Post

½″

Design 2

Ring

7/8″

1⅛″

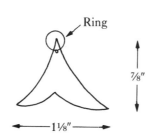

Design 3

Ring

Cherry

1⅞″

Walnut

¾″

Design 4

Walnut

Veneer

2″

Cherry

½″

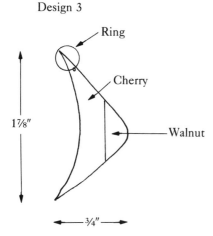

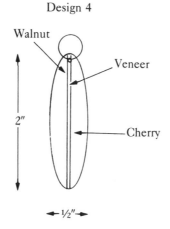

Illus. 107. Drawing of earrings.

material to a thickness of ⅛″. Using the double-face tape method described in step 3, sand both surfaces. Make designs for your earrings, and then make patterns of the designs. Trace the pattern onto the surface of the stock and cut it. Drill a 1/16″ diameter hole near the top edge. Finish the earring with lacquer. Insert a ring through the hole, and an earring wire through the ring.

33: Cutting Board (Illus. 108 and 109)

Cutting boards always make excellent gifts. While you can design the boards to resemble an animal, bird, or some other object, free-form designs are also acceptable. The design possibilities are limited only by your imagination. While hard maple is the best type of hardwood to use, you can also use oak or sycamore or another indigenous hardwood for your board.

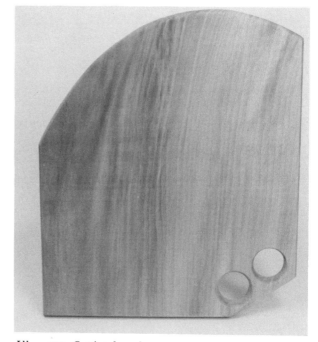

Illus. 108. Cutting board.

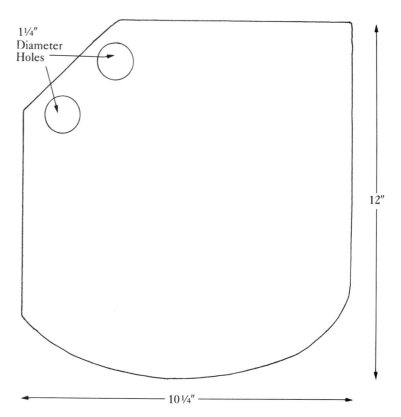

1¼" Diameter Holes

12"

10¼"

Illus. 109. Drawing of cutting board.

MATERIAL:

- 1" (4/4's) thick hardwood
- Mineral oil

TOOLS:

- Band or sabre saw
- Electric drill and bit (1¼")
- Table-mounted router and roundover bit
- Finishing sander

DIRECTIONS:

1. Design a cutting board. Use the project dimensions as a guide. Saw the board, as designed, using either a band or sabre saw.

2. If hanging or decorative holes are part of the design, drill them using the appropriate tools. With some hardwoods, you may prefer using a drill press and a multi-spur bit for drilling tasks.

3. Rout all edges using a table-mounted router and a roundover bit. Test the depth of cut using a piece of scrap. You may want to rout the edges of any holes drilled in the board. This gives them a more finished appearance.

4. Go over all surfaces with a finishing sander and various abrasive grits.

5. Finish the cutting board with several coats mineral oil. If the wood is warm, the oil will be absorbed more quickly.

34: Nut Picks

(Illus. 110 and 111)

A set of nut picks with turned hardwood handles would look good near the Christmas nut bowl. This is a project that can be made with scrap hardwood. It also gives you a chance to practise your spindle-turning on the lathe.

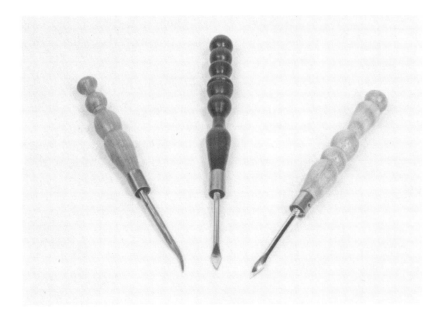

Illus. 110. Nut picks.

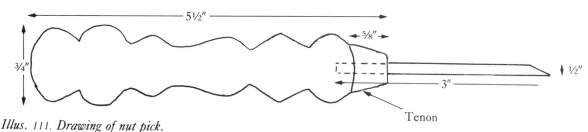

Illus. 111. Drawing of nut pick.

MATERIAL:
- 1″ (4/4's) thick hardwood
- Chrome nut picks
- ½″ diameter brass tubing
- Lacquer

TOOLS:
- Wood lathe and turning tools
- Electric drill and bit (⅛″)
- Hacksaw
- File

DIRECTIONS:

1. Prepare a series of turning blanks, approximately 1″ (4/4's) square and 6″ long. Use scraps for the blanks.

2. Secure the blanks between a prong drive center and a revolving center on the lathe. Note the suggested length and diameter of the tenon as indicated in Illus. 111. Using a vernier caliper, check the internal diameter of the brass ring and turn the tenon accordingly. Turn some fancy handles.

3. Using a hacksaw, cut the bottom 3″ off a nut pick. File a slight taper to the shaft, so that it will insert easily into the handle tenon. Check the diameter of the shaft. With a drill bit of the same diameter, probably ⅛″ or ³⁄₁₆″, drill a hole in the handle tenon. Make sure that the hole is drilled straight. The hole should be at least ⅝″ deep.

4. With the hacksaw, cut a piece of brass tubing to the same length as the handle tenon. Tap it onto the tenon and file them both flush.

5. Using a mallet or a block of wood, tap the pick into the hole in the tenon. Take your time, so that the pick does not bend or split the tenon.

6. Punch several indentations into the brass ring using a nail. These indentations hold the ring in place.

7. Finish the handle using a clear lacquer.

35: Shorebird 3

(Illus. 112 and 113)

Here is another species of shorebird—one with a radical bill. Refer to the earlier shorebird presentations in Gift Projects 4 and 13. The directions given in these earlier projects will help you in making this one. While basswood is the best wood to use for the project, pine blanks glued to thickness are also another option.

MATERIAL:

- 3″ (12/4's) thick basswood
- ¼″ diameter dowel
- ⅛″ diameter dowel
- Firewood log

TOOLS:

- Band saw
- Electric grinder
- Large tungsten carbide burrs
- Carving or sloyd knife
- Electric drill and bits (¼″ and ⅛″)
- Electric finishing sander

DIRECTIONS:

1. Use either a self-made pattern drawn on construction paper or draw the shorebird outline, to size, on the surface of the basswood.
2. Using a ¼″ wide blade on a band saw, cut the traced shorebird from the block.
3. With a knife, remove wood and rough-shape the bird. Refer to Illus. 112 and 113 to note the shape.
4. Using the electric grinder and a large burr, do the final shaping of the bird.
5. Use the electric finishing sander, with 100-grit abrasive paper, to remove markings made by the burr and do any final shaping. Prepare the surface for finishing.
6. Approximate the location of the eyes and make holes using a nail or punch.
7. Cut a slice of log about 1¾″ thick and 5″ in diameter.

8. Drill a ¼″ diameter hole in the center bottom of the bird and in the top center of the log slice. The holes should be at least ¾″ deep. Cut a piece of ¼″ diameter dowel approximately 10″ long and insert it into the bird and support base.
9. Drill a ⅛″ diameter hole at the mouth of the bird. The hole should be at least ½″ deep. Cut a 5″ long piece of ⅛″ diameter dowel; sharpen one end, bend the dowel in the center, and glue the other end into the mouth hole of the bird.
10. Finish the bird using several coats of lacquer. Rub the surface, between coats, with fine-steel wool (0000). A final coat of paste wax and a good polishing gives an excellent finish to the bird.

Illus. 112. Shorebird 3.

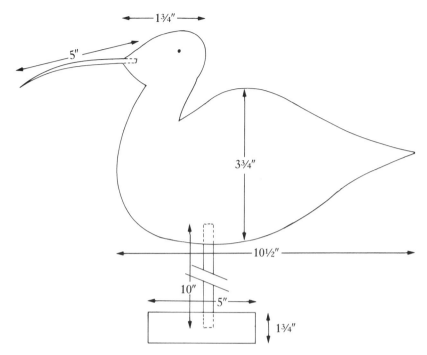

Illus. 113. Drawing of shorebird 3.

36: *Toy Horse on Wheels* (Illus. 114 and 115)

Based on an Early American design, this toy horse can be made to be pushed or pulled. With modifications to the neck, head, and ears on the design, a dog, cat, or cow can be created instead of a horse. Also, the size of the toy can be increased or decreased as desired. And, best of all, this project can be painted and decorated as desired.

MATERIAL:
- 2″ × 4″ pine
- 1″ × 4″ pine
- 1½″ diameter wheels and axles
- Rope or twine
- Paint

TOOLS:
- Sabre or band saw
- Electric drill and bit (¼″)
- Finishing sander

Illus. 114. Toy horse on wheels.

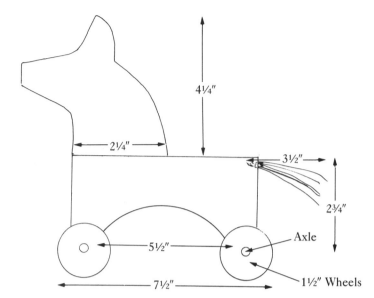

Illus. 115. Drawing of toy horse on wheels.

DIRECTIONS:

1. Make a pattern of the bottom section of the horse. Trace the pattern on a piece of 2″ × 4″ stock, and cut it out.

2. Design and make a pattern of the neck, head, and ears. Trace this pattern onto a piece of 1″ × 4″ stock. Cut out this section of the horse using a sabre, scroll, or band saw.

3. Measure and drill the holes for the wheel axles.

4. Drill a hole into the back surface, about ¼″ deep, to hold the tail.

5. Spread wood glue on the neck and the top of the body, join them together, and allow the glue to dry. If possible, clamp the parts together while the glue is drying.

6. Before assembling the axles and wheels or attaching the tail, paint the horse as desired. Allow the paint ample time to dry.

7. Using the axles and a touch of glue, secure the wheels in place. Check to see that they rotate with ease.

8. Place glue into the tail hole and force a piece of rope or twine into the hole. Unwind the threads of the rope so that it resembles a tail.

9. If a pull toy is planned, attach a small eye screw to the front surface of the body. Secure a string to the eye screw. The string can be attached to a wooden wheel, to make pulling the toy easier.

37: *Picture Holder* (Illus. 116 and 117)

This very attractive picture holder is turned and crafted from hardwood. It is designed to hold a 8″ × 10″ photograph between two pieces of glass. The glass is held in place by routed grooves in the turned posts. If you prefer, the dimensions can be modified to make a holder for a 5″ × 7″ print or any other size photograph. While the project as presented is made from black walnut, any hardwood is acceptable.

MATERIAL:
- 1½″ (6/4's) thick hardwood
- ½″ (2/4's) thick hardwood
- 8″ × 10″ pieces of window glass
- Lacquer or mineral oil

TOOLS:
- Wood lathe and turning tools
- Table-mounted router and ³⁄₁₆″ straight bit and roundover bit
- Electric drill and bit (¾″)

DIRECTIONS:
1. Cut two 1½″ (6/4's) square turning blanks that are at least 7½″ long. Blanks of this length will

Illus. 116. Picture holder.

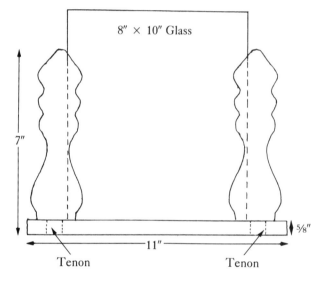

8" × 10" Glass

7"

11"

5/8"

Tenon   Tenon

Top View of Base

Tenon Hole   Tenon Hole

4½"

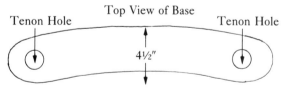

Routed Area to Hold Glass

3/16"
Wide
1/4"
Deep

Top View of Posts

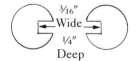

provide ample wood for turning between centers.

2. Using a table-mounted router and a ³⁄₁₆″ diameter straight bit, rout a groove in both blanks. The groove should be in the center of one side of the blanks, and run their full length. Rout the groove at least ³⁄₁₆″ deep. These grooves will hold the two pieces of glass in place.

3. Secure the blanks in the lathe and turn them. Turn a tenon on one end of each blank that is ¾″ in diameter and ½″ long. The length of the tenon is determined by the thickness of the base. Use a vernier caliper to turn the tenons to diameter. Do some fancy turning on the two posts.

4. Make a pattern of the base according to the suggested design and dimensions. Trace the pattern onto ½″ thick stock and cut out the base.

5. Rout the edges of the base using a roundover bit in the table-mounted router.

6. Place the posts on the base. This has to be done very carefully, to ensure that the glass will fit perfectly between the two posts. A number of methods can be used to accomplish this task. While holding the glass in place between the two posts, place the assembly on its side with the tenons over the base. Mark the center of the tenons on the base. These marks indicate where the ¾″ holes need to be drilled into the base to hold the tenons.

Another method that can be used is to measure the length between the centers of the tenon while the glass is in place. Transfer this measurement to the base surface, and mark where the holes are to be drilled.

7. Drill the two tenon holes through the base. Spread wood glue on the tenons and tap them into the base holes. Make sure that the routed grooves face inward and are aligned to hold the glass. Slide the glass in place to check their alignment.

8. Finish the holder using either lacquer or oil.

Illus. 117 (left). Drawing of picture holder.

75

38: Mug Holder

(Illus. 118 and 119)

This is an ideal gift for the coffee-mug collector or for those who work in an office and need a place to hang their mugs. The holder can be made to accommodate almost any number of mugs. While the holder shown in Illus. 118 and 119 has commercial mug pegs, standard dowels can be used. The woodturner, if so inclined, can spindle-turn the center post. Others may prefer making a square post from a piece of 2″ × 4″ stock. You have lots of options with this project, including whether to paint, stain, or add lacquer or oil to it.

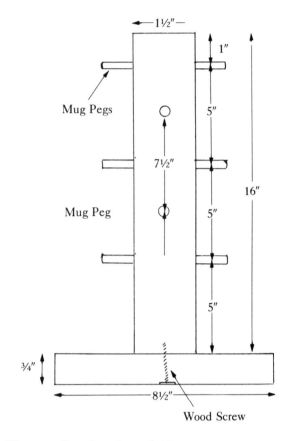

Illus. 119. Drawing of mug holder.

Illus. 118. Mug holder.

MATERIAL:
- 2″ × 4″ pine
- 1″ × 10″ pine
- Mug pegs or dowels
- Wood glue
- Wood screw
- Paint or other finishing products

TOOLS:
- Sabre or band saw
- Electric drill, bit (½″), and countersink
- Table-mounted router and roundover bit
- Finishing sander

DIRECTIONS:
1. Measure and cut or turn the center post to length. If a 2″ × 4″ stud is used, cut the post 1½″ square.

2. Using a school compass, make a circle-cutting line on the surface of a pine board. The diameter of the base needs to be large enough to support, without tipping, the post when it is full of mugs. Cut the base as traced with the compass.

3. Rout the edges on both the post and the base with a roundover bit.

4. Measure and mark, on all four sides of the post, the location of the mug pegs. There needs to be sufficient space between the pegs so that the mugs do not bang into one another when hanging. Note from Illus. 119 how the pegs are staggered on two sides. Measure the location of the pegs carefully.

5. If the pegs have ½″ diameter tenons, drill ½″ diameter holes at the points marked on the post. Make sure that the holes are deep enough to accommodate the entire tenon.

6. Using a wood screw and glue, secure the post to the center of the base. The point made by the compass is the center of the base. Use a countersink to make a small area to accommodate the head of the screw.

7. Spread glue on the peg tenons and tap them into the drilled holes in the post. Allow the glue to dry.

8. Paint or finish the mug holder as desired.

39: *Pencil Holder* (Illus. 120 and 121)

For the desk or kitchen counter, a pencil holder is almost a mandatory item. An exceptional gift can be made if the holder is turned from a scrap piece of hardwood. For those who lack a lathe, the holder can be cut square or rectangle and the pencil area can be drilled. The size of the holder can also be varied. If you're so inclined, a pencil holder may afford you the chance to do some tole painting or wood burning. It's the kind of project that lends itself to some decorative touches.

MATERIAL:
- 3″ (12/4's) thick hardwood
- Lacquer or oil

Illus. 120. Pencil holder.

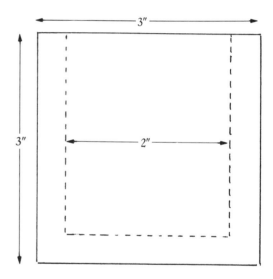

Illus. 121. Drawing of pencil holder.

TOOLS:
- Wood lathe and turning tools
- Band saw and ¼″ blade
- Drill press and 2″ multi-spur bit
- Finishing sander

DIRECTIONS:
1. Prepare a turning block to the desired dimensions. The size of stock available should determine the size of the project. For example, if you

have a piece of scrap that, when turned, would hold several pencils, use it.

2. If you plan to turn the project, use a glue block and faceplate. Turn the holder as desired. If you want, turn the inside area using a square-nose scraper. Another option is to use a multi-spur bit in the tailstock.

3. For those who do not have a lathe, cut a block square or rectangle to the desired dimensions. If you want, rout the edges with a table-mounted router.

4. Use a drill press and a 2″ multi-spur bit to drill the pencil-holding area.

5. Prepare all surfaces for finishing.

6. Finish and decorate the holder as desired.

40: *Ice Breaker*

(Illus. 122 and 123)

An ice breaker is always a welcome gift for the kitchen or the basement bar. A woodturner can make this project from scrap oak, hard maple, or another hardwood. While you may want to add a few coves or beads, the basic baseball bat design as shown in Illus. 123 and 124 is always well received. A lip has to be included on the handle section of the breaker. This, of course, is to prevent the breaker from slipping from the user's hand. A non-toxic mineral oil makes a good finish.

MATERIAL:
- 2″ (8/4's) thick hardwood
- Mineral oil

TOOLS:
- Wood lathe and turning tools

DIRECTIONS:
1. Cut a 2″ square turning block so that it's approximately 13″ long. Scrap can be used. Modify its dimensions according to the scrap available.
2. Secure the blank between a prong center and a revolving center. Turn as desired.
3. Finish the breaker with a non-toxic oil.

Illus. 122. Ice breakers.

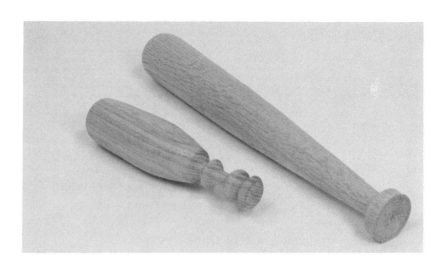

Illus. 123. Drawing of ice breaker.

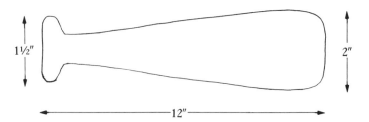

41: Doll Cradle

(Illus. 124 and 125)

Doll cradles are mandatory gifts for little girls, especially if they are granddaughters. This project was designed for a young lady named Mallory. You may have to measure the doll to determine the appropriate size of the planned cradle. There is sufficient surface on its ends and sides for a variety of painted or stencilled decorations. This is a fun project to make and decorate, especially if there are young helpers available.

MATERIAL:
- 1″ × 10″ pine board
- 1″ × 8″ pine board
- Finishing nails
- Wood glue
- Paint

TOOLS:
- Sabre, band, table, or radial arm saw
- Table-mounted router with roundover bit
- Finishing sander

DIRECTIONS:
1. Refer to Illus. 125 for the cradle's design and dimensions. Make a full-size pattern of the end section of the cradle. Trace the pattern on the 1″ × 10″ stock and cut it out. Remember, two end sections have to be made.
2. Measure and cut the two side pieces. Refer to Illus. 125 and make the full-size bottom piece.
3. Rout all edges except those on the bottom piece and the side edges that attach to it.
4. Using the finishing sander and a fine-abrasive grit, prepare all surfaces for finishing. Make sure that there are no sharp edges or possible splinters on the surfaces.
5. With wood glue and finishing nails, assemble the two sides and the bottom piece. Using a nail set, drive the nail heads under the surface.
6. Center the bottom/side section on the inside surface of one end piece. Using wood glue and finishing nails, secure the end piece to the assembled section. Tap the nail heads under the surface.
7. Measure and mark the second end piece for securing to the assembled section. It needs to be attached exactly as the first piece, or the cradle will not rock properly. Secure the second end piece with wood glue and finishing nails. Use a nail set to drive the nail heads under the wood's surface.
8. Paint and decorate as desired. You may want to consider putting a name or two on the cradle.

Illus. 124. Doll cradle.

Side View   End View   Top View

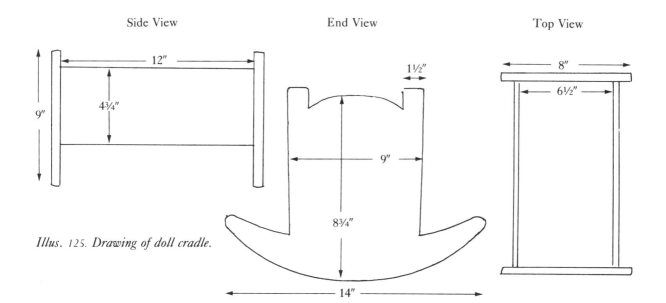

Illus. 125. Drawing of doll cradle.

42: *Lapboard* (Illus. 126 and 127)

This is the ideal gift for someone who likes to sit in a comfortable chair and write letters, do homework, or some other task. The project shown in Illus. 126 and 127 was developed by Peter Jacobson for use as an undergraduate student, and is made from black walnut. Use an attractive piece of hardwood. The size of the lapboard should, in part, be determined by the hardwood used. Given the amount of hardwood involved in the project, you will put extra effort into finishing the board.

MATERIAL:
• 1″ (4/4's) thick hardwood
• Lacquer or mineral oil

TOOLS:
• Sabre or band saw
• Table-mounted router and roundover bit
• Finishing sander

DIRECTIONS:
1. Measure and cut the board to the dimensions indicated in Illus. 127.

2. Lay out the inset area as suggested in Illus. 127 and cut it.

3. Rout all edges using a roundover bit.

4. Using a variety of abrasive grits and a finishing sander, prepare the surfaces and edges for finishing.

5. Finish the board using either a clear-lacquer or oil finish. Spend extra time on the finishing.

Illus. 126. Lapboard.

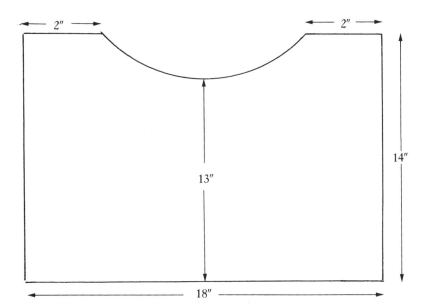

43. Painted Bowl

(Illus. 128 and 129)

Turned bowls that are painted make unusual and very attractive gifts. Bowls are normally finished with a clear-lacquer or oil finish, especially those turned from an attractive piece of hardwood. You can, however, turn bowls from pine or less attractive and expensive hardwoods and paint them. There are many paints on the market, including those used in auto-body work, that can be used on bowls. The bowl can be finished in either traditional or radical colors.

MATERIAL:
- 2¼″ (9/4's) thick hardwood or softwood
- Paint

TOOLS:
- Band saw and ¼″ blade
- Wood lathe and turning tools
- Finishing sander

DIRECTIONS:
1. Cut a turning block to the desired diameter. If you prefer, glue together several boards of hardwood such as pine to achieve the desired thickness.

Illus. 128. Painted bowl.

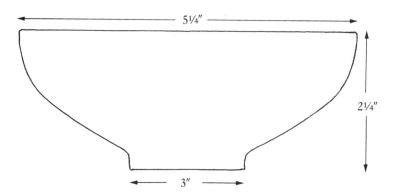

Illus. 129. Drawing of painted bowl.

5¼"

2¼"

3"

2. Prepare a glue block and secure it to the bottom surface of the bowl block. Attach a faceplate and secure it to the lathe. Turn the block to the desired shape.

3. You may have to use some abrasive paper on the turned bowl while it is still on the lathe. Prepare the surfaces for painting.

4. Paint the bowl as desired. High-gloss enamels can be used to make a very attractive bowl. Check the label regarding possible need for a primer. Allow ample time between coats of paint for adequate drying.

44: Candle Holders

(Illus. 130 and 131)

The design for this project can be used to make candles for either a formal or informal setting. Best of all, the candles can easily be hung on a wall. Commercial candle cups are used, which greatly enhance the project. Also, there's lots of surface for decorative painting or stencilling.

MATERIAL:
- 1" × 4" pine
- Candle cups
- Wood glue
- Finishing nails
- Paint

TOOLS:
- Sabre, scroll, or band saw
- Table-mounted router and roundover bit
- Electric drill and bit, or countersink
- Finishing sander

DIRECTIONS:
1. Measure and cut the two back pieces and the two support pieces to length. Note from looking at Illus. 131 that the support pieces are not as wide as the back pieces.

2. From construction paper, make a pattern of

Illus. 130. Candle holders.

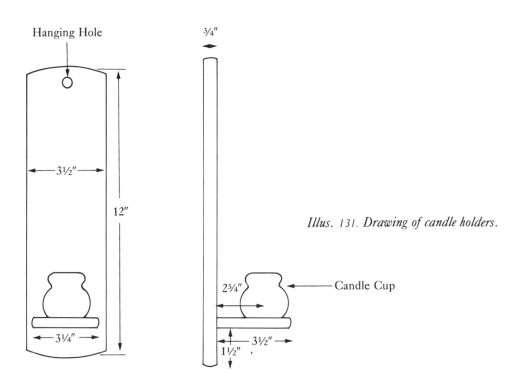

Front View   Side View

Hanging Hole   ¾″

3½″

12″

Illus. 131. Drawing of candle holders.

2¾″   Candle Cup

3¼″

3½″

1½″

the curve that is needed for both ends of the back piece and the front end of the support piece. See Illus. 130 for the shape of the curve.

3. Trace the curve on all ends and cut it.

4. Rout all edges except the back of the support pieces. These are joined to back pieces and should not be routed.

5. Measure and drill hanging holes using a drill/countersink.

6. Glue and clamp the candle cups on the front edge of the two support pieces. You may also want to drive a small finishing nail from the bottom of the support piece into the cup.

7. Prepare all surfaces for finishing.

8. Measure and mark the location of the support pieces on the front surface of the back pieces. Spread glue on the back edges of the support pieces and nail them in place. The nails should be driven through the back pieces and into the support pieces. Allow the glue to dry.

9. Paint and decorate as desired.

45: Heart Box

(Illus. 132 and 133)

This Early American box can be used in a variety of ways. It is large enough to hold magazines, and, if used with a divider, it could also hold fruit or something similar. And if the receiver of the gift enjoys gardening, it makes a very functional tool or seed box. The box shown in Illus. 132 is painted red.

MATERIAL:

- ½″ × 8″ pine
- ½″ × 4″ pine
- Wood glue
- Finishing nails
- Paint

TOOLS:

- Sabre, band, scroll, table, or radial arm saw

Illus. 132. Heart box.

Side View

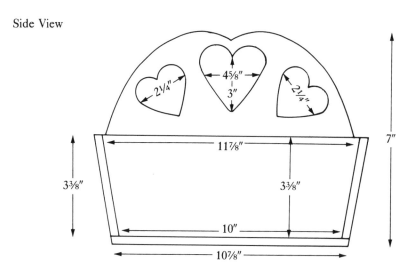

Illus. 133. Drawing of heart box.

End View

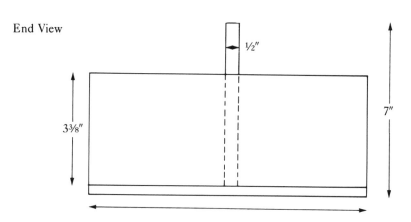

- Table-mounted router and roundover bit
- Finishing sander
- Electric drill and bit (¼″)

DIRECTIONS:

1. Review Illus. 132 and note the overall design of the box. If you are unable to obtain ½″ thick pine and do have access to a planer, use standard ¾″ thick stock. If stock of a standard thickness is used, you will have to slightly modify some of the dimensions.

2. Measure and cut the two side pieces. Use the top and bottom measurements given in Illus. 132 to make the needed angle.

3. Measure and cut the two end pieces.

4. Using a wider board, lay out the box center-piece. Note the dimensions given in Illus. 132. The sides of the centerpiece are cut to this same angle as the side pieces of the box. Make the two curves on the top edge meet in the center of the piece.

5. Make heart patterns from construction paper and trace them onto the surface of the center piece. Drill a hole through the traced heart pattern with a ¼″ diameter bit. This will allow you to thread a sabre or scroll-saw blade through the hole in order to cut out the heart. Cut all three hearts using these procedures.

6. Rout all edges except those that attach to other boards. Also rout both sides of the hearts.

7. Using wood glue and finishing nails, assemble the two side pieces and the two end pieces. Check Illus. 132 to verify how they should be assembled.

8. Measure and mark the location of the center-piece. Use wood glue and finishing nails to secure it in place. Drive the head of all nails under the surface using a nail set.

9. Measure the bottom area of the box and cut sufficient boards to cover it. This is a good area on which to use scrap material. Glue and nail the boards in place.

10. Go over all surfaces with a finishing sander and a fine-grit abrasive paper. Wipe off all dust.

11. Paint and decorate the box.

46: Animal/Bird Key Holders (Illus. 134 and 135)

Key holders are inexpensive, easy to make, and always useful. Once you make a few of the suggested designs, you will begin to develop your own designs for key holders. Best of all, they can be made from pieces of hardwood scraps. Key chains are available in a variety of lengths and colors. While an oil finish is quick and easy, you may want to paint and decorate a few of the holders.

Illus. 134. Animal/bird key holders.

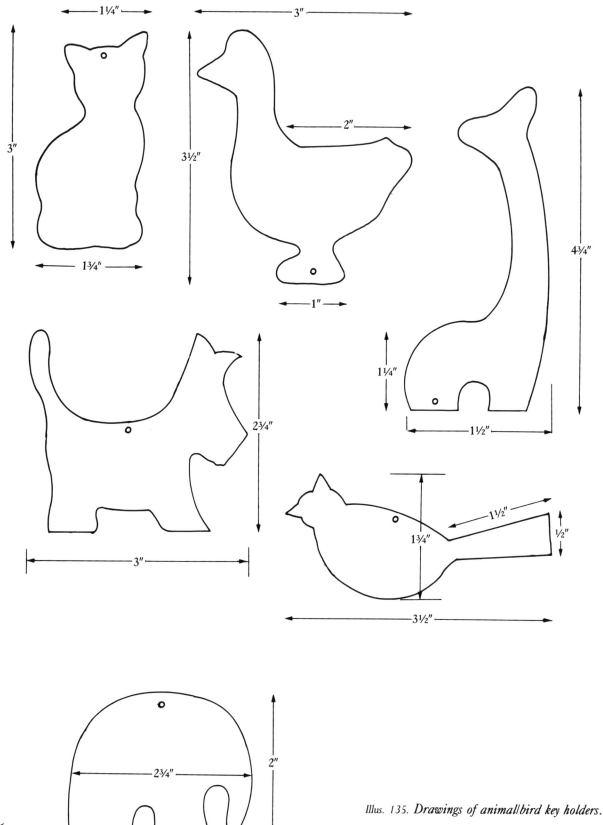

Illus. 135. *Drawings of animal/bird key holders.*

MATERIAL:

- ⅜″ thick hardwoods (scraps)
- Key chains
- Oil

TOOLS:

- Scroll or sabre saw
- Electric drill and ⅛″ bit
- Finishing sander

DIRECTIONS:

1. While key holders can be made of any design, you may want to begin with those detailed in Illus. 135. Make patterns of each design from construction paper.

2. Trace the patterns on scrap hardwood material and cut them using either a scroll or sabre saw. If a sabre saw is used, use a finishing blade. You may also have to clamp the scrap pieces, to make cutting them easier and safer.

3. Drill an ⅛″ diameter hole in the key holders to accommodate a key chain. Refer to Illus. 134 to note the placement of the chain holes.

4. Prepare the surfaces for finishing either using an electric sander or sanding by hand.

5. Apply oil to finish the holders. When they are dry, insert a key chain through the drilled hole.

47: Hanging Plant Holder (Illus. 136 and 137)

In an age when windowsills are fast becoming a thing of the past, hanging plant holders have become a necessity. For the person who enjoys potted plants, a plant holder will be appreciated. The design permits the holder to be easily secured to a wall or at the end of a cabinet. Also, the pot-holding piece can be varied in size to accommodate different diameter pots. If you're so inclined, you may want to paint the holder and decorate its surface. A clear-lacquer finish also looks good.

MATERIAL:

- 1″ × 8″ pine
- 1″ × 4″ pine
- Eye screw
- Wood screws
- Hook
- Macrame rope
- Lacquer or paint

TOOLS:

- Sabre or scroll saw

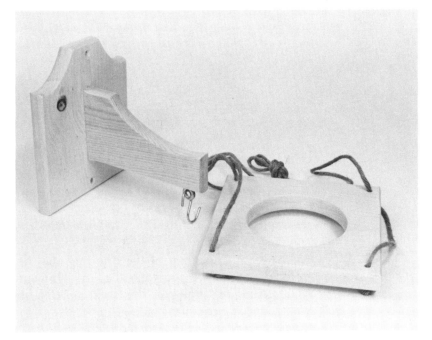

Illus. 136. Hanging plant holder.

Front View: Back Piece and Arm

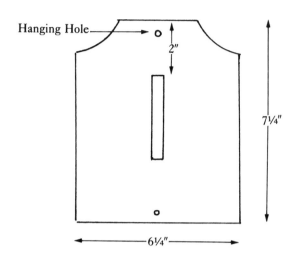

Hanging Hole

2"

7¼"

6¼"

Side View: Back Piece and Arm

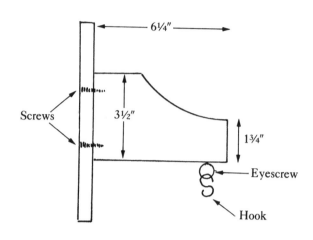

6¼"

Screws

3½"

1¾"

Eyescrew

Hook

Top view: Pot Holder

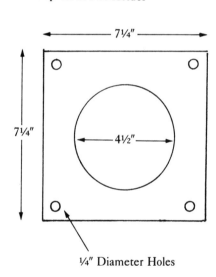

7¼"

7¼"

4½"

¼" Diameter Holes

Side View: Pot Holder

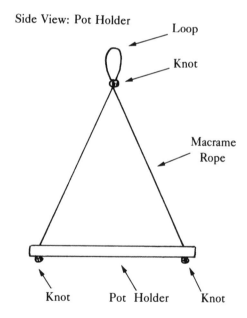

Loop

Knot

Macrame Rope

Knot

Pot Holder

Knot

Illus. 137. Drawing of hanging plant holder.

- Drill press or electric drill and ¼" bit
- Countersink or electric drill and bit
- Circle cutter
- Table-mounted router and roundover bit

DIRECTIONS:

1. Measure, trace the patterns for, and cut the back piece and the arm. Refer to both Illus. 136 and 137 for assistance.

2. With the exception of the arm end that attaches to the back piece, rout all edges. Drill and countersink two holes in the back piece, with which to hang the plant holder.

3. Using wood glue and wood screws, center and

secure the arm to the front surface of the back piece.

4. Measure and cut the pot-holder section to the dimensions indicated in Illus. 137.

5. If a drill press and circle cutter are available, cut a 4½″ diameter hole in the pot holder section. This diameter will accommodate a standard flower pot. If a larger or smaller pot is to be used, vary the hole diameter accordingly. The hole can also be cut using a school compass and a sabre saw. Drill a hole for the blade to penetrate.

6. Rout all edges on the pot-holder section.

7. Measure and drill ¼″ diameter holes at each corner of the pot-holder section. These holes will accommodate the macrame rope used to hang the pot holder.

8. Prepare all surfaces for finishing. Apply either a clear-lacquer finish or paint and decorate.

9. Secure an eye screw to the bottom edge of the arm. Slip a metal hook through the eye of the screw.

10. Cut two 40″ long pieces of macrame rope. Thread the ends of the rope through the drilled holes in the pot-holder section. Tie knots on each end to prevent the rope from slipping back through the drilled holes.

11. In order to hang the rope on the hook, tie the two ropes together, leaving a loop about 2″ long. Make certain that the ropes permit the pot-holder section to hang straight.

48: Necktie Holder (Illus. 138 and 139)

For the man with many ties, a necktie holder can be a much-needed gift. Both the size and design of the tie holder can be modified to meet individual needs. Best of all, attractive tie pegs are available to use for the holder. If you prefer, cut and use standard dowels. The holder is designed to be screwed to a closet wall or door.

MATERIAL:
- 1″ × 4″ pine
- Tie-rack pegs
- Screw-hole buttons
- Paint or lacquer

TOOLS:
- Sabre or scroll saw
- Electric drill and ³⁄₁₆″ and ½″ bits
- Table-mounted router and roundover bit
- Finishing sander

DIRECTIONS:
1. Design and measure the back section of the tie holder. Refer to Illus. 139 to note both the size of the back section and the distance between the tie pegs. A pattern from construction paper may be useful in your design process.

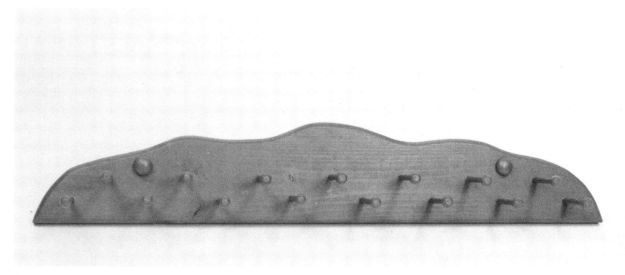

Illus. 138. Necktie holder.

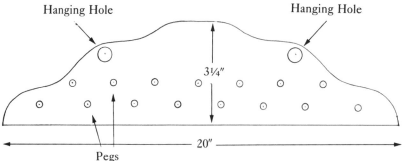

Illus. 139. *Drawing of necktie holder.*

Hanging Hole

Hanging Hole

3¼"

20"

Pegs

2. Trace or draw the back-section design onto a piece of 1″ × 4″ pine stock. Cut out the design.
3. Rout all edges.
4. Measure and mark the location of the tie pegs. Allow at least 2½″ between the pegs if you have two staggered rows of pegs. There should be ample room for the ties to hang.
5. If tie-rack pegs are to be used, drill ³⁄₁₆″ diameter holes at each marked location. Drill the holes to a depth of at least ¼″. The depth of the holes should be the same for all the pegs.
6. Measure and mark the two hanging holes. Refer to Illus. 139. If screw hole buttons are to be used, note that their tenon is often ½″ in diameter. Drill two holes that will accommodate the button tenons. These buttons cover the head of the screws and make for a more attractive project.
7. Using a nail or splinter of wood, place wood glue in each tie-peg hole and tap the peg in place. Wipe off any excess glue.
8. Prepare the surface for finishing, and finish the project with either paint or lacquer. Remember to finish the top of the screw hole buttons.

49: *PJ's Back Scratcher*

(Illus. 140 and 141)

For the person you think has everything, this uniquely designed back scratcher will prove to be a welcomed gift. Designed by P. J. O'Neill and turned by Andy Matoesian, it requires a minimum of effort to use, but provides a maximum of scratching comfort. The design eliminates the necessity of reaching over your shoulder to scratch. Best of all, the back scratcher is a desktop item that can be used in the office. It will also give you the opportunity to do spindle-turning.

MATERIAL:
• 1″ (4/4's) thick black walnut
• Lacquer or mineral oil

TOOLS:
• Wood lathe and turning tools
• Vernier caliper
• Electric drill and ½″ bit

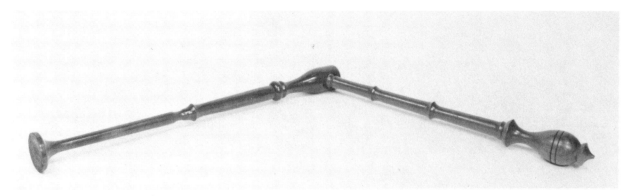

Illus. 140. *PJ's back scratcher.*

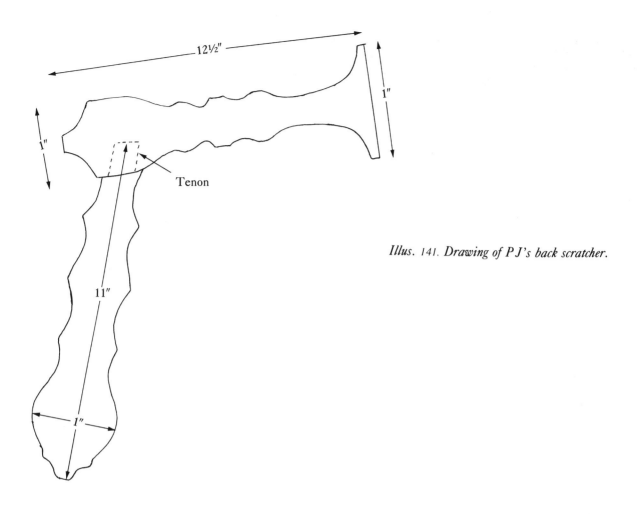

12½″

1″

1″

Tenon

11″

1″

Illus. 141. Drawing of P J's back scratcher.

DIRECTIONS:

1. Refer to Illus. 141 and prepare the turning spindles to their appropriate length and thickness. While black walnut was used for the back scratcher shown in Illus. 140 and 141, other hardwood can be used. Hopefully, there are scraps available that can be used for this project.

2. Secure the handle spindle between a drive center in the headstock and a revolving center in the tailstock. Refer to Illus. 140 for ideas on turning the handle. A ⅝″ long, ½″ diameter tenon must be turned on one end of the handle. This tenon is inserted, at an angle, into a drilled hole in the scratching arm. When it has been turned, prepare the spindle for finishing.

3. Secure the arm spindle in the lathe and turn

it. Refer to Illus. 140 and 141 to note how the scratching end of the arm is designed. When the arm spindle has been completely turned, prepare it for finishing.

4. Using a ½″ diameter wood bit, drill a hole, at a slight angle, near the bottom end of the arm spindle. Refer to Illus. 140 or 141 to note the approximate location. The hole should be at least ⅝″ deep, or deep enough to accommodate the tenon.

5. Spread wood glue in the drilled hole and insert the tenon. Wipe away any excess glue, and allow the glue to dry.

6. Finish the project using either a clear lacquer or oil.

50: Corner Shelf

(Illus. 142 and 143)

Corner shelves, especially small ones, are hard to find. They are ideal for displaying a small, treasured collectible in a protected space. This one was designed and crafted by Wendell Meyer.

While the shelf can be made from one of the hardwoods, pine that is either painted or lacquered looks very attractive.

MATERIAL:
- 1″ × 6″ pine
- Sawtooth hangers
- Finishing nails and wood glue
- Paint or lacquer

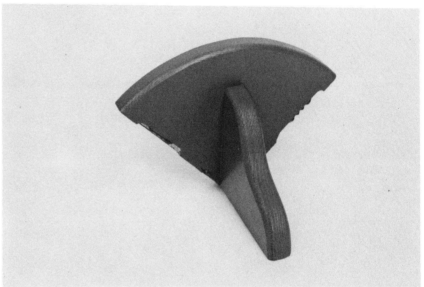

Illus. 142. Corner shelf.

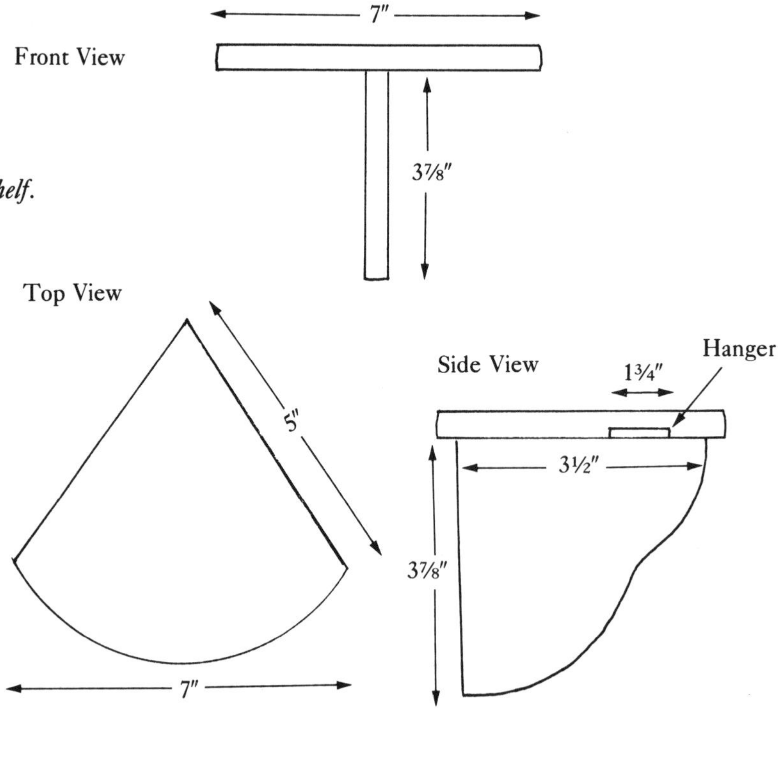

Illus. 143. Drawing of corner shelf.

Front View

7″

3⅞″

Top View

5″

7″

Side View

Hanger

1¾″

3½″

3⅞″

TOOLS:

- Scroll or sabre saw
- Table-mounted router with roundover and rabbeting bits
- Finishing sander
- School compass

DIRECTIONS:

1. Refer to Illus. 143 and prepare patterns for both the top piece and the shelf support. A school compass can be helpful in making the curved area of the top piece. If you prefer, the shelf can be easily enlarged.

2. Trace the patterns onto the surface of the wood and cut them. You may want to consider making several shelves. They use very little wood.

3. Using a roundover bit, rout the two edges of the curved area of the top piece. Also, rout the front two edges of the support piece.

4. With a rabbeting bit, rout two areas on the sides of the top piece for the sawtooth hangers. Refer to Illus. 143 for the location of the hangers. The routed area should be deep enough to accommodate the hanger.

5. Prepare all surfaces for finishing.

6. Using wood glue and finishing nails, assemble the top piece to the support piece. The back edges of the support piece should be even with the bottom edges of the top piece. This will allow a small triangular section of the top piece to extend beyond the support.

7. Finish the shelf with either a clear lacquer or paint.

8. Nail the sawtooth hangers in place.

51: *Punched Copper Pineapple* (Illus. 144 and 145)

Here is an unusual gift: a punched copper pineapple, symbolizing welcome, secured in a hardwood frame. These kinds of projects are great fun to make because they involve using a variety

Illus. 144. Punched copper pineapple.

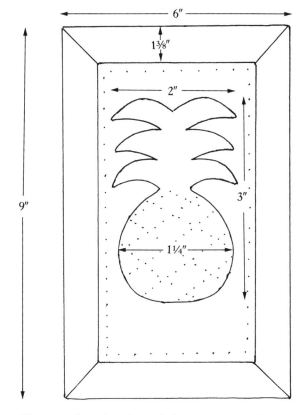

Illus. 145. Drawing of punched copper pineapple.

of materials and different skills. Once you discover how easy it is to work with copper, you may want to make and frame other designs. As you might guess, the size of the project can be increased or decreased, as desired.

MATERIAL:
- 1" (4/4's) thick wild cherry
- Sheet of copper
- Liver of sulphur
- Rubber bands (No. 105: 5" long, ⅝" wide)
- Clear lacquer

TOOLS:
- Mitre saw
- Table-mounted router with roundover and rabbeting bits
- Sharp punch
- Finishing sander

DIRECTIONS:
1. To assist you in making the project frame, refer to Gift Project 2. Use the dimensions given in Illus. 145 when making the frame. When routing the frame, remember that the rabbet area should only be the thickness of the copper.

2. While wild cherry was used for the project shown in Illus. 144, a different hardwood can be used. If possible, use scrap.

3. When the frame is made, finish it with a clear lacquer or an oil finish.

4. Measure the inside dimensions of the rabbeted area of the frame. Cut a piece of copper to these dimensions. (Sheets of copper are often available at local craft stores or by mail order.) Usually kitchen scissors will cut copper.

5. Using an alcohol pen, draw the pineapple design on the surface of the copper. Mistakes can be removed with a damp tissue.

6. Place the sheet of copper on a scrap piece of wood and, using a sharp punch, make holes along the lines of the pineapple drawing. Make the holes uniform in size. The distance between the holes should be approximately the same. You may want to refer to Illus. 144 or 145.

7. Make a boarder of punched holes approximately ¼" from the inside edges of the frame. Place the copper in the frame and then mark, with the pen, the location of the boarder.

8. Rub liver of sulphur on the front surface of the copper. This solution gives the copper an old, shaded appearance. Be certain to read the label directions and cautions on the liver of sulphur. You may prefer leaving the copper natural looking. If, however, sulphur is used, allow it to dry. Rub the copper with steel wool to remove some of the black effect of the sulphur. Wipe the surface of the copper clean.

9. Measure and cut a piece of construction paper that will fit over the back of the frame. Spread a small bead of white glue in the rabbeted area of the frame and set the copper in place. Glue the construction paper onto the back of the frame and allow the glue to dry.

10. Use either hanging holes or a sawtooth hanger to hang the finished project.

52: Child's Step Stool

(Illus. 146 and 147)

For the person who needs a few more inches to reach something, a step stool will prove helpful. If you prefer, the stool can be made both lower and wider, to give added stability. Made from pine, this project can be painted or decorated. The stool has ample surface on which to express your creativity.

MATERIAL:
- 1" x 8" pine
- 1" x 4" pine
- Flattop screw-hole plugs
- Wood screws
- Paint

TOOLS:
- Sabre, scroll, band, or table saw
- Electric drill or drill press and ½" wood bit
- Table-mounted router and roundover bit
- Finishing sander

Illus. 146. Child's step stool.

Front View

Wood screw   Wood screw

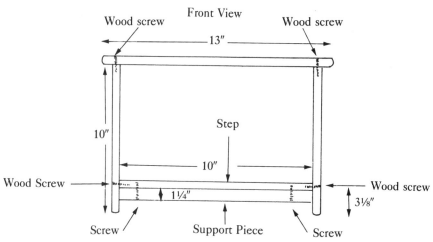

13″

Step

10″

10″

Wood Screw   Wood screw

1¼″   3⅛″

Screw   Support Piece   Screw

Illus. 147. Drawing of child's step stool.

Side View

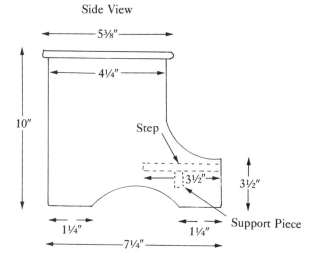

5⅜″

4¼″

10″

Step

3½″   3½″

1¼″   1¼″

Support Piece

7¼″

DIRECTIONS:

1. Using Illus. 147 as a guide, measure and cut the various parts. In all, there are five parts to the stool: the top, the two side pieces, the step, and the support piece.

2. With the exception of the support piece, rout the edges of all the parts using a roundover bit. Do not rout edges that will attach to other parts.

3. Measure and mark the location of screw holes on the top piece. Four screws, two on each side, should be used to secure the top piece to the two side pieces. Using a ½″ diameter wood bit (if you are using ½″ diameter screw-hole plugs), drill the four holes, as marked. The drilled holes should be at least ½″ deep.

4. Measure and mark the location of screw holes on the outside surface of the sides. Two screws should be used on each side to secure the step. Note the placement of the step in both Illus. 146 and 147. The holes should be the same diameter as the screw plugs, and about ½″ deep. Do not drill holes for the support piece yet.

5. Prepare all surfaces for finishing using a sander.

6. Using wood glue and screws, assemble the two sides to the step. When the step is in place, assemble the top piece to the sides using screws and glue. Place a spot of glue in the screw holes and tap a screw plug in place. The plugs should be flush with the surface.

7. Drill two ½″ diameter holes into one edge of the support piece. The holes should be at least ½″ deep, and approximately 2½″ from the ends of the piece. Screws will be drilled through these holes and into the bottom of the step.

8. Center the support piece under the step and secure it to the side pieces. Measure and mark on the outside surfaces of the side pieces the location of screw holes for the support piece. Drill the holes deep enough to accommodate the screw plug.

9. Secure the support piece, under the step, to the side pieces using wood glue and screws. Spread a bead of glue on the support-piece edge that touches the bottom surface of the step. Also, secure the support piece to the step with screws

through the holes in the bottom edge. Spread a spot of glue in the screw holes and tap in the plugs. Allow the glue to dry.

10. If necessary, using a finishing sander, sand any screw-hole plugs that are protruding so that they are flush with the surface.

11. Paint and decorate the step stool.

53: *Spalted Scoop/Spoon*

(Illus. 148 and 149)

For those who like truly exotic wood, carve them a project made of spalted wood. Spalted wood is the result of fungal infestation. The wood is in an early state of rot, and develops very attractive black lines. The lines are called black zone lines, and they form a network of patterns that are both unusual and attractive. Spalted wood is somewhat softer and thus easier to carve or shape than regular wood.

While spalted wood can be purchased at some hardwood dealers, your best source is the woodpile. Look at the ends of logs for the tell-tale black zone lines. If it is wet, allow the wood to dry in the garage for several months before using it. The scoop/spoon is a decorative piece but can be used in a nut dish or bowl.

MATERIAL:
- 2″ (8/4's) thick spalted wood
- Lacquer

TOOLS:
- Band saw
- Electric grinder
- Large tungsten carbide burrs
- Moto Tool with sanding sleeves
- Finishing sander
- Sloyd or carving knife

DIRECTIONS:

1. If you find a spalted log, saw a 2″ thick carving block from it with a band saw. Cut the block to

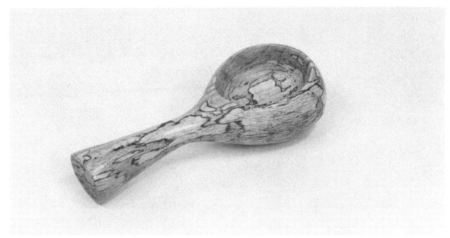

Illus. 148. *Spalted scoop/spoon.*

Top View

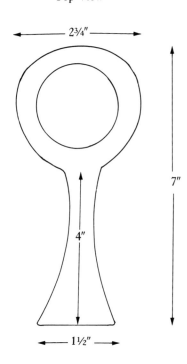

2¾"

7"

4"

1½"

Illus. 149. *Drawing of spalted scoop/spoon.*

Side View

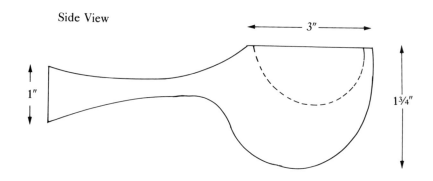

3"

1"

1¾"

97

the dimensions suggested in Illus. 149, or to larger dimensions.

2. Draw the pattern for the scoop/spoon on the surface of the carving block, and cut it out using a band saw. Also use the band saw to remove some of the excess wood on the handle. Refer to Illus. 148 or 149 to note how the project is shaped.

3. Remove wood and shape the project using a grinder and burrs. If a grinder and burrs are not available, use a sloyd or carving knife. If available, use a scorper to remove wood from the spoon area of the project. A Moto Tool and sanding sleeves can also be used.

4. Use an electric sander to prepare the surfaces for finishing. You will have to hand-sand the inside area of the spoon.

5. Finish the project with a clear lacquer. Because spalted wood is rather porous, several coats of lacquer will be required. Rub the finish with steel wool (0000) between applications. Remove the dust and wool hairs from the surface before applying another coat of lacquer.

54: *Message/Reminder Board* (Illus. 150 and 151)

Every household can use a message board. This one has a pine frame, a sheet of cork 8½" x 11" and ³⁄₁₆" thick that can be purchased at a local craft store or ordered from a mail-order supplier, and a piece of plywood to support the cork. The board can be enlarged or reduced in size to meet a particular need. The frame can be painted and decorated or stencilled.

MATERIAL:
• 1" x 4" pine
• Sheet of cork (8½"x 11")
• ⅛" thick plywood
• Finishing nails and wood glue
• Sawtooth hanger
• Paint

TOOLS:
• Band saw

Illus. 150. Message/reminder board.

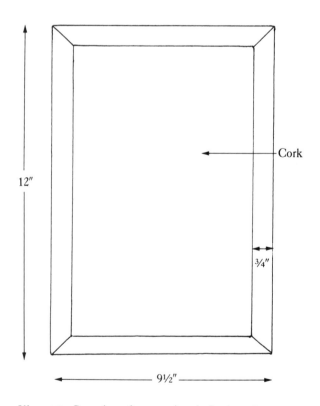

Illus. 151. Drawing of message/reminder board.

- Mitre saw
- Table-mounted router and roundover and rabbeting bits
- Finishing sander

DIRECTIONS:

1. Using a band saw, prepare the frame materials to the dimensions suggested in Illus. 151. If you have scrap pieces of pine, use them rather than cut into a new board.

2. With a rabbeting bit, rout the bottom inside edges of the frame. The rabbet should be at least ⅜″ deep, so several passes must be made with the router. Do not try to rout the area in one pass. Observe all safety precautions when using the router. This area must accommodate both the sheet of cork and the plywood.

3. Rout the other edges of the frame material with a roundover bit.

4. Mitre the frame sections to their proper dimensions.

5. Assemble the frame using wood glue and small finishing nails. You also may want to use large rubber bands to help assemble the frame. Refer to Gift Project 2 for ideas on assembling a frame. Use a nail set to drive the heads of the nails under the surface of the wood.

6. Measure and cut a piece of ⅛″ thick plywood to the same dimensions as the sheet of cork. Both have to fit into the rabbeted area of the frame.

7. Before gluing the cork and plywood into the frame, paint the frame.

8. Glue both the cork and the plywood into the frame using wood glue. Spread only a small bead on the edge of the rabbeted area. Too much glue will squeeze out and onto the surface of the cork.

9. Center and nail a sawtooth hanger or similar hanging device on the back of the frame.

55: Candle Holders (Illus.

152 and 153)

Always a fun project to make and paint, candle holders are a well-received gift, especially around the Christmas season. This project, made from pine, can use either commercially made candle cups or those turned from dowels. The size of the project can also be varied to meet a particular need. The holders can be painted (red?) and decorated for the holiday season. Candles are easily obtained to fit the commercial cups.

MATERIAL:
- ½″ thick pine
- 1″ x 4″ pine
- Candle cups (1″ high, with ½″ hole)
- Wire brads and wood glue
- Paint

TOOLS:
- Scroll or sabre saw
- Finishing sander
- School compass

DIRECTIONS:

1. Make a pattern of the holder body using construction paper. Make sure that the three arms are exactly the same. The dimensions given in Illus. 153 can be used as such, or modified if you prefer.

2. Trace the pattern onto the surface of ½″ thick pine stock. If you don't have ½″ thick material, resaw pine of standard thickness on a band saw. If available, a planer would do a better job, and do it more quickly. You may find ½″ thick stock at a lumberyard.

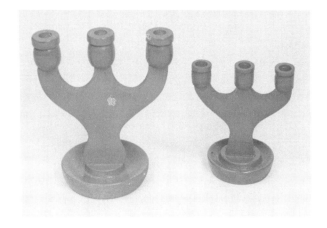

Illus. 152. Candle holders.

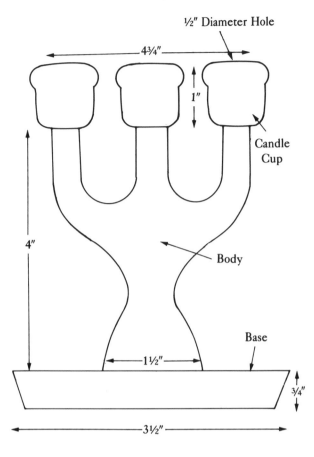

½" Diameter Hole

4¾"

1"

Candle
Cup

4"

Body

Base

1½"

¾"

3½"

Illus. 153. Drawing of candle holder.

3. Using a school compass, trace a 3½" circle on a piece of scrap or 1" x 4" pine. This will serve as the base for the holder. Cut out the base.

4. Sand all surfaces and edges using fine-grit abrasive paper. Round over the edges slightly with the abrasive paper. Wipe off all the sanding dust.

5. Using wood glue and wire brads, center and secure the candle cups to the three arms. Drive the brads into the base of the candle cups, leaving a portion of the brad extending. With abrasive paper or a file, sharpen the head of the brad. Spread glue on both the arm and the cup, and force the brad into the arm. Allow the glue to dry.

6. Spread glue on the bottom edge of the body, and nail the two parts together, from the bottom of the base.

7. Paint and decorate the project.

56: *Shorebird 4*   (Illus. 154

and 155)

Here is another shorebird with a totally different design. This one is made from two pieces of basswood, or another wood of choice, that are joined together with a dowel. Refer to the earlier shorebird projects for additional ideas on making these birds.

MATERIAL:
• 3" (12/4's) thick basswood
• ½" dowel
• Lacquer

TOOLS:
• Band saw
• Electric grinder
• Large tungsten carbide burrs
• Carving or sloyd knife
• Palm-handled carving tools
• Electric drill and ½" bit
• Electric finishing sander

DIRECTIONS:
1. Prepare a rough block for the neck and head section based on the finished dimensions given in Illus. 155. The open bill can be cut during this task.

2. Draw the pattern for the body of the bird and cut it out. Remove as much wood as possible with the band saw.

3. Drill a ½" diameter hole, at least ¾" deep, into both the bottom of the neck piece and the top of the body. Refer to Illus. 154 and 155 to note both the placement and angle of the holes.

4. Cut a piece of ½" diameter dowel to a length of 1½". Spread glue in the drilled holes and on the surfaces where the neck and body will make contact. Tap the dowel into the hole in the body and force the neck piece around the protruding section. Make sure that the neck and body surfaces contact each other securely. Allow the glue to dry.

5. Remove wood and shape the neck and body

Illus. 154. Shorebird 4.

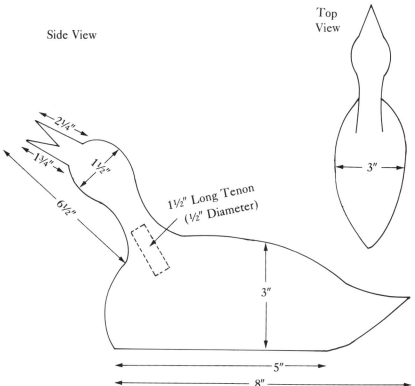

Side View

Top View

2¼"

1¾"

1½"

6½"

1½" Long Tenon
(½" Diameter)

3"

3"

5"

8"

Illus. 155. Drawing of shorebird 4.

sections using the tools available. Refer to Gift Project 4 for some ideas on making shorebirds.

6. Do the final shaping and surface preparation with an electric finishing sander and a variety of abrasive papers.

7. If desired, using palm-handled or other carving tools, add feather detail to the tail section of the bird. You may also want to make markings on the bill. The tips of wings can be indicated by a carved triangle and a few carved lines indicating feathers. Use your imagination. Remember, this is but an approximation of a shorebird.

8. Finish the bird with several coats of a clear lacquer. Go over the surface with steel wool (0000) between coats. Remove any dust and hair before applying another coat of lacquer. Rub in paste wax to create a good final finish.

57: Candle Shelf (Illus. 156 and 157)

This candle shelf, created from ½″ thick pine, features an Early American design. A candle holder can be set on the top shelf, and a personal treasure can be displayed on the bottom shelf compartment. Best of all, if you're so inclined, this shelf can be significantly increased in size.

MATERIAL:
- ½″ thick pine
- Finishing nails and wood glue
- Paint

TOOLS:
- Scroll or sabre saw
- Band saw
- Table-mounted router and roundover bit
- Electric drill and countersink drill
- Finishing sander

Illus. 156. Candle shelf.

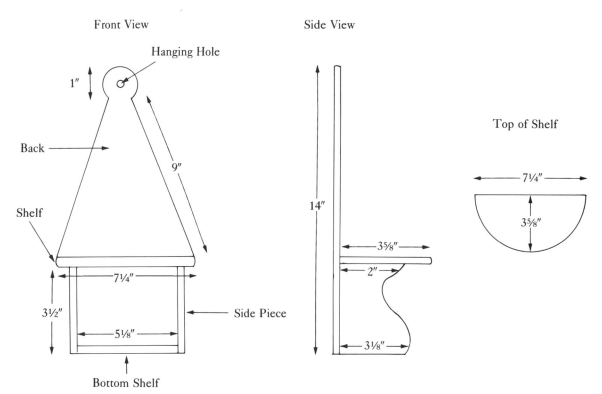

Illus. 157. Drawing of candle shelf.

102

DIRECTIONS:

1. The back piece of the shelf should be laid out, to the dimensions indicated in Illus. 157, on the surface of ½″ thick stock. Refer to Illus. 157. If you are going to make the shelf larger than the dimensions indicated, you may want to use standard 1″ (¾″ thick) pine. Cut out the back piece.

2. Using Illus. 157 as a guide, make patterns of both the side pieces and the top shelf. Trace the patterns on the stock and cut them. Remember, two side pieces are needed.

3. Measure and cut the bottom shelf using the dimensions given in Illus. 157.

4. Slightly round over all edges that will not attach to another piece when the project is assembled. For example, the back edges of the top shelf should *not* be routed because they will attach to the surface of the back piece.

5. Drill and countersink a hanging hole in the rounded area at the top of the back piece.

6. Sand all surfaces in preparation for finishing.

7. Assemble the two side pieces and the bottom shelf using wood glue and finishing nails.

8. Attach with glue and nails the side pieces/bottom shelf assembly to the front surface of the back piece.

9. Glue and nail the top shelf to the back piece and also to the side pieces. Allow the glue to dry.

10. Paint and decorate the project.

58: *Matchbox with Drawer* (Illus. 158 and 159)

This fireplace matchbox will make a useful gift whether or not there is a fireplace in the home. It can be used to display dried flowers or pussy willows. The small drawer can be used for a box of matches or as a place to hide something small and precious. The matchbox can be stained and lacquered or, if you prefer, painted and decorated. The wood used for the box is called batting. Most lumberyards stock it. Buy 2½″ wide batting that is ⅜″ thick. You will also need a short piece of 2″ batting that is ¼″ thick.

MATERIAL:

- 2½″ batting (⅜″ thick)
- 2″ batting (¼″ thick)
- Small brass knob
- Finishing nails and wood glue
- Paint or stain and lacquer

TOOLS:

- Scroll or sabre saw
- Radial arm or band saw
- Table-mounted router and roundover bit
- Electric drill and bit or countersink
- Finishing sander

DIRECTIONS:

1. With the exception of the drawer, each part of this project needs a pattern. Make patterns for the back, the sides, and the front, using Illus. 159 as a guide.

Illus. 158. Matchbox with drawer.

103

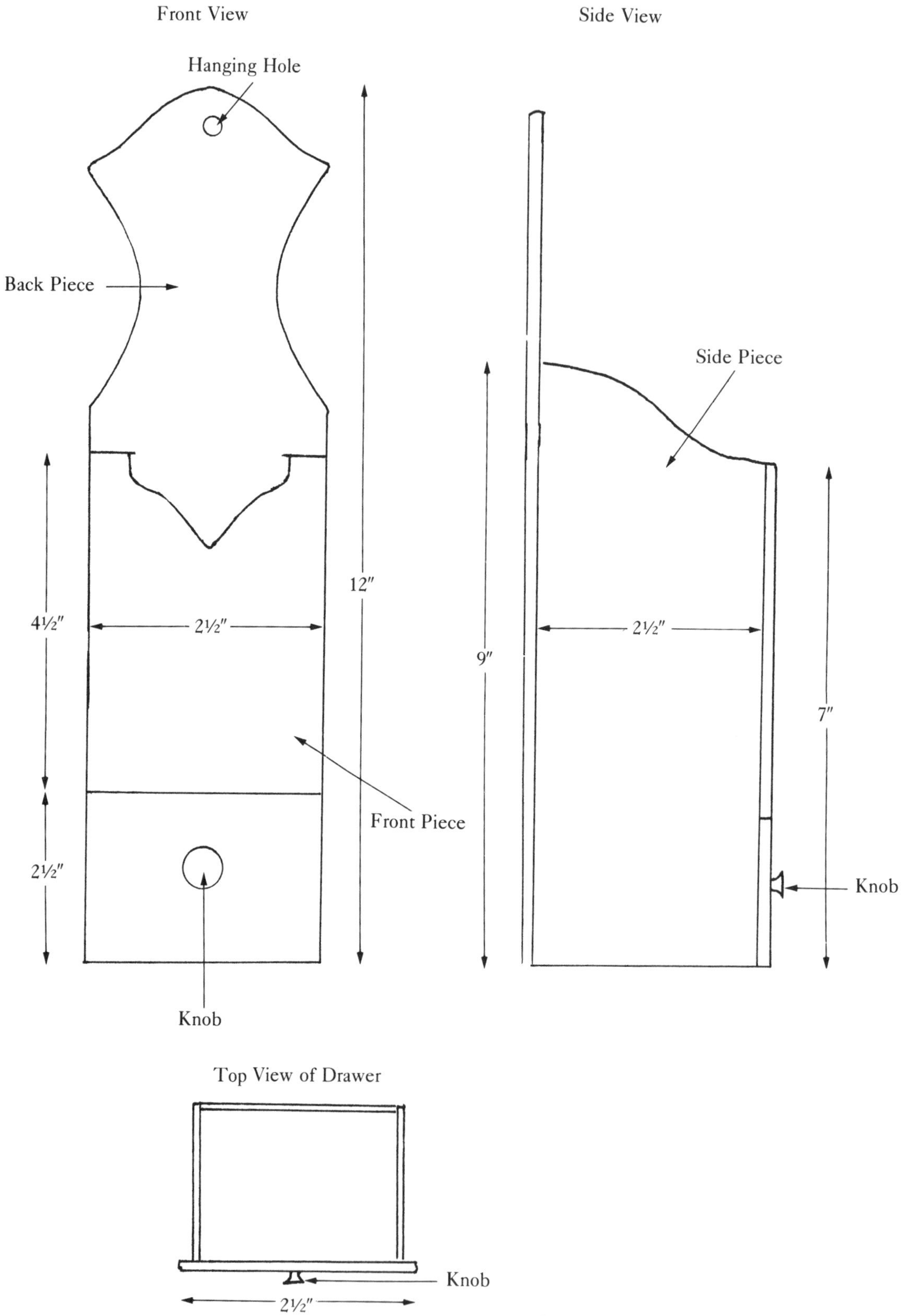

Front View

Hanging Hole

Back Piece

12"

4½"

2½"

2½"

Knob

Side View

Side Piece

9"

2½"

7"

Knob

Front Piece

Top View of Drawer

Knob

2½"

Illus. 159. Drawing of matchbox with drawer.

2. Trace the patterns on the surface of the batting and cut out the various parts. Remember to make two sides.

3. With a roundover bit, rout all edges except those that will attach to another part.

4. Measure and drill, using a countersink and drill, the hanging hole in the top area of the back piece.

5. Using a finishing sander, prepare all surfaces for painting or staining. Remove all dust.

6. Assemble the box using wood glue and small finishing nails. With a nail set, drive the nail heads under the surface of the wood. Wipe away any excess glue. If you plan to stain the box, sand off any glue that may have accumulated on the surface. Stain will not take on the parts of the surface where glue remains.

7. Measure and cut the front piece of the drawer. You may want to refer again to Illus. 159. Round over all edges with the router.

8. Measure the inside depth and height of the box and cut the two drawer side pieces. These pieces should be cut, if possible, from batting that is 2″ wide and ¼″ thick.

9. Place the two side pieces in the drawer area and measure the distance between them. Cut a piece to this length that will serve as the back piece of the drawer.

10. Using wood glue and small brads, assemble the drawer. You may want to use rubber bands to clamp the assembly while the glue dries.

11. Measure the bottom area of the drawer and cut a piece that will fit inside. This piece will serve as the bottom for the drawer.

12. Glue and nail the bottom piece in place.

13. Stain and lacquer or paint the box.

14. Secure a small brass knob to the center front of the drawer.

59: *Leanne's Knitting Needles* (Illus. 160 and 161)

For those who enjoy knitting or would like to learn, what could be a better gift than custom-turned needles made from black walnut? These needles were designed by Leanne DeLaurenti. Unable to find the kind and quality of knitting needles she preferred, Leanne asked Andy Matoesian, a friend, to turn needles to her specifications. The results are the needles shown in Illus. 160. Though black walnut adds a certain amount of pizzazz to the needles, a different hardwood can also be used.

MATERIAL:
- ¾″ thick black walnut
- ⅜″ diameter black walnut dowels
- ¼″ diameter black walnut dowels
- Lacquer

TOOLS:
- Wood lathe and turning tools
- Collet or four-jaw chuck
- Key chuck for tailstock, and ¼″ and ⅜″ bits

DIRECTIONS:
1. Prepare turning blocks for the handles that are at least 4″ long. If a chuck is used, you will want to turn tenons that will be used to hold the block in place while turning it.

As you will note from Illus. 160 and 161, the handles for the two sizes of needles are different. The handles for the same size needles, however, should be the same size and have the same design.

Illus. 160. Leanne's knitting needles.

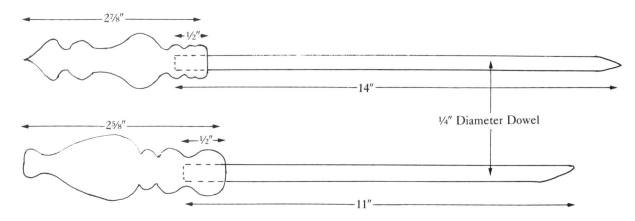

Illus. 161. Drawing of Leanne's knitting needles.

2. Secure a block in the chuck and turn a tenon. Reverse the block, secure the tenon in the chuck, and turn the handle. The top portion of the handle should be nearer to the chuck. The bottom end of the handle will be drilled using a chuck and bit secured in the tailstock.

3. Drill a ⅜″ diameter hole, at least ½″ deep, into the bottom of the handles for the larger needles. Use the tailstock with the key chuck and bit secured in it for this task. For the smaller needles, drill a ¼″ diameter hole to the required depth.

4. While the handle is on the lathe, separate the handle from the tenon. Catch the handle as it separates so that it doesn't get damaged.

5. Cut the ⅜″ and ¼″ diameter dowels to their respective lengths. Refer to Illus. 161 for the dimensions.

6. Place some wood glue into the handle hole and insert the appropriate size dowel. Repeat this process for all the needles. Wipe off any excess glue and allow the glue to dry.

7. To turn the points on the needles, insert them through the headstock spindle and chuck. Allow several inches of the dowel to extend beyond the chuck, and secure it in place. Turn the tapered point. The taper should be about 1″ long. Refer to Illus. 160 and 161 to note how the points should be made.

8. Finish the needles with a clear-lacquer finish. Rub the needles with steel wool (0000) between coats. A final coat of paste wax, rubbed well, will give the needles an excellent finish.

60: *Painted Flowers* (Illus. 162 and 163)

If you have a friend who likes flowers but lacks either the space or energy to grow them, this is the ideal gift. Painted wood flowers can be set in the yard any time of the year. They can also be placed in a pot of dirt in the house to add a touch of color and a reminder of spring. While the flowers shown in Illus. 162 and 163 are approximations of tulips, any flower can be duplicated in wood. Made from pine, the flowers can be painted in a variety of colors, including a green stem and leaves.

MATERIAL:
- Scraps of pine
- ¼″ diameter dowels
- Paint

TOOLS:
- Sabre or scroll saw
- Electric drill and ¼″ bit
- Finishing sander

DIRECTIONS:
1. Design and make a pattern of the flower. As indicated, you may want to use a different flower than the project tulip.

2. Trace the flower pattern onto scrap pieces of pine and cut it.

Illus. 162. Painted flowers.

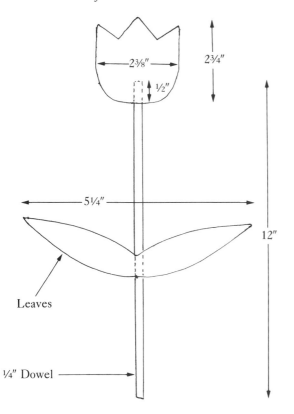

2³⁄₈″

2³⁄₄″

¹⁄₂″

5¹⁄₄″

12″

Leaves

¹⁄₄″ Dowel

Illus. 163. Drawing of painted flower.

3. Either freehand or with another pattern, make the leaf section. Make two leaves from one piece of scrap. Refer to Illus. 162 or 163.

4. Drill a hole approximately ½″ deep into the base of the flower.

5. Drill a hole through the leaf section in the center of the two leaves.

6. Cut a ¼″ diameter dowel to a length of 12″.

7. Glue the dowel into the base of the flower. Slip the leaf section onto the dowel and glue it. Allow the glue to dry.

8. Paint the project, using green for the stem and leaves.

61: *Checkerboard* (Illus. 164 and 165)

A great deal of work is involved in making this gift, but it will be much appreciated if given to someone who enjoys playing checkers or collects game boards. The board is made from squares of black walnut and wild cherry. The frame around the squares is from the same woods.

The wood checkers, one set natural and the other walnut, can be ordered from several mail-order suppliers.

MATERIAL:
- ⅜″ thick black walnut
- ⅜″ thick wild cherry
- ¼″ thick plywood
- ¼″ diameter dowel
- 12 small wood screws
- 1 set walnut checkers
- 1 set natural checkers
- Wood glue
- Lacquer

TOOLS:
- Band saw and ½″ blade
- Mitre saw
- Electric drill and ¼″ and ¹⁄₃₂″ bits
- Clamps
- Finishing sander

Illus. 164. Checkerboard.

Top View

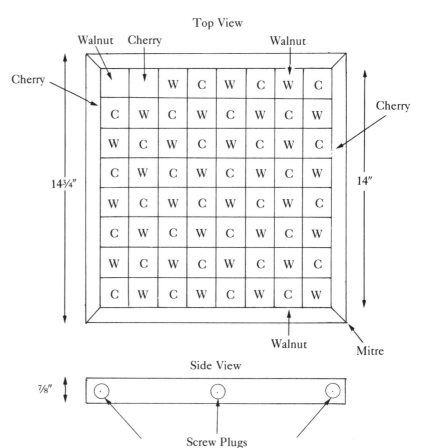

Walnut   Cherry   Walnut

Cherry

		W	C	W	C	W	C
C	W	C	W	C	W	C	W
W	C	W	C	W	C	W	C
C	W	C	W	C	W	C	W
W	C	W	C	W	C	W	C
C	W	C	W	C	W	C	W
W	C	W	C	W	C	W	C
C	W	C	W	C	W	C	W

Cherry

14¾″   14″

Illus. 165. Drawing of checkerboard.

Walnut   Mitre

Side View

⅞″

Screw Plugs

DIRECTIONS:

1. Set the fence of the band saw to cut 1¾″ squares. Cut 32 black-walnut squares and 32 wild-cherry squares. You may want to cut a few extra squares of each wood just in case. It's important that the squares are all the same dimension. If you don't have walnut or cherry, use other contrasting hardwoods. If the wood is slightly thicker or thinner than ⅜″, it will work just fine.

2. Measure and cut two pieces of ¼″ thick plywood exactly 14″ square. Sixty-four 1¾″ squares will fit perfectly on the plywood. The second piece is used for clamping the glued squares.

3. Place the squares on the plywood. This is similar to laying a tile floor. Pay careful attention to how the wood grain runs. The grain on all the walnut squares should run in one direction. The grain on all the cherry squares should run in the opposite direction.

Spread an even coat of wood glue on an outer section of the plywood. Do only two rows of squares at a time. When these rows are done, then spread more glue. Start the process with a corner square. Refer to Illus. 165 to note the assignment of the squares.

Take your time with this procedure. Make sure that the squares are perfectly aligned with the outside edge of the plywood. Squeeze the squares together to eliminate any space between them. Wipe off, with a warm, damp cloth, any glue that may have squeezed onto the surface. Put down all the squares.

4. Spread sheets of wax paper over the glued squares and place the second piece of plywood on the paper. Clamp the two pieces of plywood together, thus pressing the glued squares tightly against the surface. If any of the squares squeeze out of place, tap them back. The wax paper will prevent the clamping piece of plywood from being glued to the surface of the squares. A certain amount of glue always squeezes out during the clamping process. Leave the assembly clamped until the glue is dry.

5. Remove the clamps and tear off the wax paper. A certain amount always sticks to the surface. Using a finishing sander and fine-grit abrasive papers, prepare the surface for finishing. Be sure to remove any excess glue that may remain. Work carefully when preparing the surface.

6. Measure and cut out a mitred frame. The frame surrounds the board and is screwed to the plywood. Two pieces of the frame should be from black walnut, and the other two from cherry. Refer to Illus. 165 for dimensions and placement of the screw holes.

7. Drill three ¼″ diameter holes ³⁄₁₆″ deep into each of the frame pieces. The holes should be placed in the same location on each frame piece. The holes will hold the head of the wood screws and a plug.

8. With the ¹⁄₃₂″ bit, drill through the center of each ¼″ hole. This pilot hole will prevent the screw from cracking the frame.

9. Using wood glue and small screws, attach the frame, one section at a time, to the edges of the plywood. Make sure that the mitres are aligned at each corner before screwing the frame piece in place. The frame will extend at least ⅛″ above the board's surface. This, of course, will prevent the checkers from sliding off the board. It also makes for a more attractive board.

10. Cut 12 plugs ⅛″ long from the ¼″ diameter dowel. Put a spot of glue in each frame screw hole and tap a plug in place. The plugs should be flush with the surface of the frame.

11. Sand the edges of the frame with fine-grit abrasive paper, by hand. Be careful not to scratch the surface of the board. The sides of the frame can be sanded with an electric sander.

12. Apply several coats of clear lacquer to all surfaces of the board. Rub each coat with steel wool (0000) and then wipe the surface clean of dust and hairs. Apply several coats of paste wax to the board's surface, and polish it.

13. Sign the bottom of the board with your name and the date. This adds a nice touch.

62: Executive Shooting Range (Illus. 166 and 167)

For diversion, fun, and relief from stress, a shooting range that uses rubber bands may be the ideal gift. As you might guess, *this gift is not recommended for children.* Both the pistol and the target employ spring clothespins in their design. The pins hold small targets. When the targets are hit, the pins revolve on a dowel.

MATERIAL:
- 1″ x 4″ pine
- ½″ diameter dowel
- ⅛″ diameter dowel
- Wooden beads (⅛″ diameter center hole)
- 4 spring clothespins
- Rubber bands
- Wood glue and wire brads
- Paint

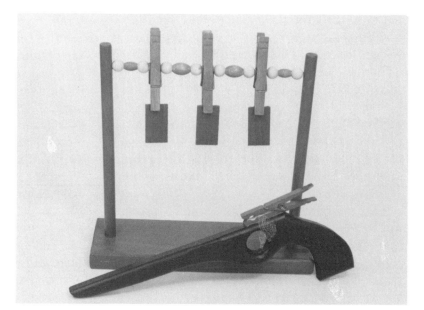

Illus. 166. *Executive shooting range.*

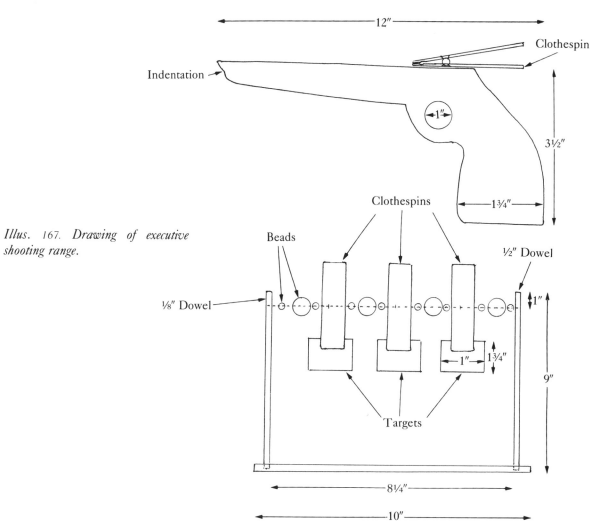

Illus. 167. *Drawing of executive shooting range.*

TOOLS:

- Sabre or scroll saw
- Band saw
- Electric drill and ¼″, ⅛″, and 1″ bits
- Table-mounted router and roundover bit
- Finishing sander

DIRECTIONS:

1. Draw a "pistol" on the surface of 1″ x 4″ pine according to the design and dimensions presented in Illus. 167. Cut out the gun. Also, cut a small indentation on the front of the gun barrel. This indentation holds one end of the rubber band when the gun is loaded.

2. Drill a 1″ diameter trigger hole.

3. Rout with the roundover bit all edges, including the trigger area.

4. Secure a clothespin to the top surface of the gun with a brad and glue. Refer to Illus. 166 and 167 to note the placement of the pin. Clamp the pin while the glue is drying.

5. Measure and cut the base of the target stand. Rout all its edges using a roundover bit.

6. Drill two ½″ diameter holes in the base. Refer to Illus. 167 for the placement of the holes.

7. Cut two ½″ diameter dowels to a length of 9″. Drill a ⅛″ diameter hole 1″ from the top of each dowel. The hole should go through the dowel.

8. Cut a 9″ long piece of ⅛″ diameter dowel.

9. Thread the beads and the three clothespins onto the ⅛″ dowel. Refer to Illus. 166 to note the results of this procedure.

10. Place the ⅛″ diameter dowel into the holes of the ½″ diameter dowel, and secure it with glue. When the rubber band strikes one of the targets, the entire clothespin and target should spin freely around on the ⅛″ dowel.

11. Spread glue in the holes in the base and insert the dowels holding the target assembly. Allow the glue to dry.

12. Using the band saw and pine scraps, cut three targets that will be secured in the clothespins. The targets should be about ⅛₁₆″ thick. Refer to Illus. 167 for other dimensions.

13. Paint the gun and target assembly. *When using this game, watch where you shoot!*

63: Plate Shelf

(Illus. 168 and 169)

A small plate shelf to display a blue plate or some other collectible can be a valuable gift. The design used for the plate shelf shown in Illus. 168 and 169 has a routed groove to hold the plate, along with a support piece which can be used to secure the shelf to a wall. The groove can be eliminated, if so desired. The shelf, given its size, can be used to display many other items. The design is such that the shelf can be made larger than expected. Paint it so that it blends in with the item(s) to be displayed.

Illus. 168. Plate shelf.

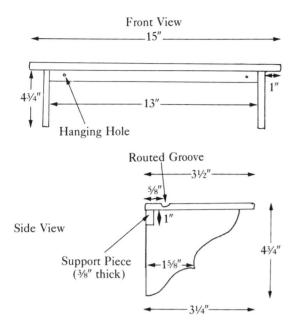

Illus. 169. Drawing of plate shelf.

MATERIAL:

- 1″ x 4″ pine
- ⅜″ thick pine
- Finishing nails and wood glue
- Paint

TOOLS:

- Sabre or scroll saw and radial arm saw
- Table-mounted router and roundover and roundnose bits
- Finishing sander
- Electric drill and countersink

DIRECTIONS:

1. Measure and cut the top piece. Refer to Illus. 169 for its dimensions.
2. Make a pattern for the two legs of the shelf. Use the dimensions given in Illus. 169 to make the pattern.
3. Trace the pattern on the stock and cut it.
4. Cut a piece of ⅜″ thick pine to the dimensions of the support piece. Drill two hanging holes in the support piece.
5. With the roundover bit, rout the edges on the top piece and the legs. Do not rout edges that will be attached to other pieces. Also, do not rout the support piece.

6. Using a fence on the router table and a ⅜″ diameter roundnose bit, rout a plate groove in the surface of the top piece. The groove should be about ¼″ deep and approximately ⅝″ from the back edge.
7. An area to hold the support pieces must be cut out of the back/top of the legs. Place the end of the support piece against the surface of the leg and trace it. Cut the area out and check it for fit. Repeat the process on the other leg.
8. Using wood glue and small finishing nails, attach the support piece to the legs. Secure this assembly to the top piece with glue and nails. Make sure that the legs are placed an equal distance from each end of the top piece. Allow the glue to dry.
9. Paint or stain and lacquer the shelf.

64: Weed Pots

(Illus. 170 and 171)

Scrap chunks of wood from the woodpile or the shop can be used to make these containers, which display weeds or dried flowers. Weed pots of different sizes and styles, and made from different woods, can be easily turned on the lathe.

MATERIAL:

- Logs or scrap material

Illus. 170. Weed pots.

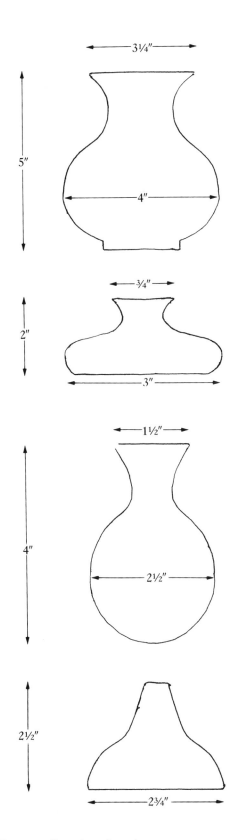

Illus. 171. Drawing of weed pots.

- Pine scrap for glue blocks
- Lacquer or mineral oil

TOOLS:
- Wood lathe and carving tools
- Band saw and ¼" blade
- Clamps
- School compass
- ½" and 1" bits
- Finishing sander

DIRECTIONS:
1. Using a school compass, draw patterns for large turning blocks, and then cut them out on the band saw.
2. Prepare pine glue blocks from scrap. Glue and clamp the turning blocks to the glue blocks. If you have one of the many commercial available chucks, use it instead of the glue blocks.
3. Attack a faceplate to the glue block, secure the glue block to the lathe, and turn it.
4. Secure a drill bit in the tailstock and drill a hole in the turned pot. The size of the pot should determine the diameter of the bit used. The hole should penetrate to within ½" of the bottom of the pot.
5. With the band saw, separate the turned pot from the glue block. Sand the bottom surface.
6. Repeat the entire process and turn a variety of pots. Experiment with their shapes and sizes, along with different woods.
7. Finish the pots with either lacquer or mineral oil.

65: *Spoon Holder* (Illus. 172 and 173)

This project would make an appropriate gift for the person who collects spoons or simply wants to display the various baby spoons and other eating utensils used over the years by his or her family. While the size of the holder can be increased, you may want to start with the suggested dimensions. The holder can be painted and decorated.

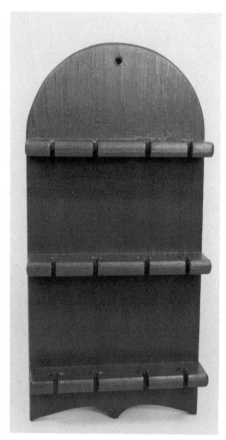

Illus. 172. Spoon holder.

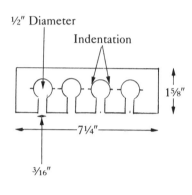

Illus. 173. Drawing of spoon holder.

MATERIAL:

- ½" thick pine
- Wood glue and finishing nails
- Paint

TOOLS:

- Sabre or scroll saw and band saw
- Table-mounted router and roundover bit
- Electric drill and ½" bit and countersink
- Moto Tool and sanding sleeves
- Finishing sander
- School compass

DIRECTIONS:

1. Measure and cut the back piece of the holder. If ½" thick pine is not available, use pine of the standard thickness.

2. Use a school compass to make the curved top on the back piece.

3. Make a pattern for the bottom design on the back piece; then trace it on the pine and cut it out.

4. Using ½" thick stock, cut three holders to the dimensions presented in Illus. 173.

5. Refer to Illus. 173 and measure and mark the location of the spoon holes on the holders. Drill ½" diameter holes at each of the marked locations.

6. Rout all edges using the roundover bit. Do not rout edges that will attach to another part.

7. Mark and saw the slots for the drilled holes on each of the holders. Note the approximate width of the slots in Illus. 173.

8. Make two indentations at each hanging hole, to ensure that the spoon will hang straight. Refer to Illus. 173 to note the location of these sanded-out areas. Either a Moto Tool with a sanding sleeve or a round wood file can be used. Experiment with a spoon and the indentations until it hangs properly.

9. Drill a hanging hole with the countersink drill bit.

10. Sand all surfaces in preparation for finishing. Wipe off the dust after sanding.

11. Using wood glue and finishing nails, attach the holders to the back piece. Refer to Illus. 173 to note where the holders should be placed.

12. Paint and decorate the holder.

66: *Desktop Message Holder* (Illus. 174 and 175)

A companion piece for some of the other desktop gifts, the message holder is a simple project to make. A round base from black walnut holds a large, brass paper clip, into which messages can be inserted. The clip is available from any number of mail-order suppliers. While the round base is best turned on the lathe, for those without this tool the base can also be made square or rectangle. The base is small enough to be made of hardwood scrap.

MATERIAL:
• ¾″ (3/4's) thick piece of hardwood
• Brass paper clip with base
• Lacquer or oil

TOOLS:
• Band saw or wood lathe and turning tools
• Electric drill and ¼″ and ⅛″ bits
• Finishing sander

DIRECTIONS:
1. Prepare the base from a hardwood using either a wood lathe or a band saw. If a square base is desired, make it approximately 3¼″ square. If you plan to turn the base, use a glue block and refer to Illus. 175.

2. Drill a ¼″ diameter hole, from the bottom, about halfway through the base. Its depth will be determined by the length of the screw that comes with the brass clip.

3. Use the ⅛″ bit to drill a hole through the

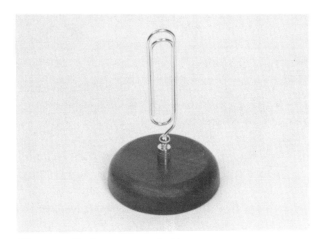

Illus. 174. Desktop message holder.

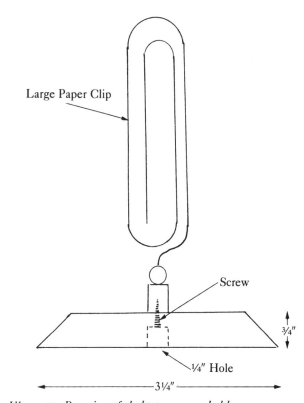

Illus. 175. Drawing of desktop message holder.

remainder of the base. This will allow the small bolt that comes with the clip to pass easily through the base. You may have to use a larger bit if the diameter of the bolt is larger than ⅛″.

4. Prepare the surfaces of the base for finishing. Wipe off the dust and apply a lacquer or oil finish.

5. Secure the paper clip to the base with the provided bolt.

115

67: Key Holder 2 (Illus. 176 and 177)

This would make a perfect gift for the individual who needs a place to store his keys. Made from pine and ⅛″ diameter dowels, the holder can be crafted to any size. While a clear-lacquer finish always looks good on pine, you may want to paint the holder and add a few flowers or some other decoration. By the way, use a wood screw to hang the holder. This makes it much easier to remove and hang the keys.

MATERIAL:
- 1″ x 10″ pine
- ⅛″ dowels
- Wood glue
- Paint, oil, or lacquer

TOOLS:
- Sabre or scroll saw
- Table-mounted router and roundover bit
- Electric drill and ⅛″ bit
- Countersink drill
- Finishing sander

DIRECTIONS:
1. Measure and draw the holder pattern on the surface of a pine board. Check Illus. 177 for the dimensions. The handle has to be centered, so be very careful when laying out the project. Cut out the holder.
2. Measure and mark the locations of the dowels. Drill ⅛″ diameter holes ¼″ deep at each location.
3. Locate and drill the hanging hole in the handle using a countersink drill.
4. Rout all edges of the holder
5. Sand the surfaces and edges. Remove all dust, especially from the dowel holes.
6. Measure and cut ⅛″ diameter dowels, 1¼″ long. For this project you will need 15 dowels.
7. Spread wood glue on scrap, dip the end of a dowel into the glue, and tap the dowel into a drilled hole. Wipe off any excess glue.
8. Finish and decorate the holder.

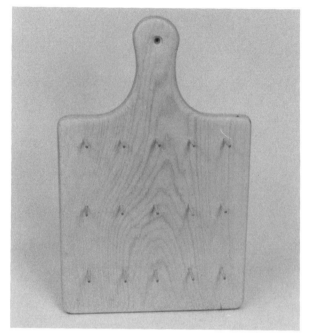

Illus. 176. Key holder 2.

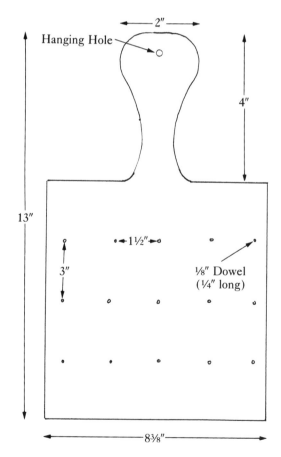

Illus. 177. Drawing of key holder 2.

116

68: *Covey of Birds* (Illus. 178 and 179)

This handsome covey of birds is not only fun to design and make, but even more fun to paint. It makes a striking display on top of the kitchen cabinet or in the corner of a room. Illus. 178 and 179 offer design ideas, but don't be afraid to try your own.

MATERIAL:
- 1″ x 6″ pine
- ¼″ thick dowels
- Fireplace logs
- ⅛″ thick dowels
- Paint

TOOLS:
- Sabre or scroll saw
- Band saw
- Electric drill and ⅛″ and ¼″ bits
- Finishing sander

DIRECTIONS:
1. Make a pattern of each bird using the approximate dimensions in Illus. 179 as a guide. Also refer to Illus. 178 and 179 for design ideas. While you may simply want to draw the bird design on the wood, patterns really help.

2. Trace the patterns on the wood and cut them out.

3. Find some logs on the woodpile and cut bases for each of the birds. Bases that are 3″ in diameter and at least 1″ thick should support the birds.

4. Drill ¼″ diameter holes in the bottom edge of each bird and in the center of the bases. Depending upon the desired position of the bird (for example, eating), the hole should be drilled at an angle.

5. Cut a ¼″ diameter dowel to an appropriate length for each bird.

6. For those birds that will have a dowel for a bill, drill a ⅛″ diameter hole in the head area. The hole should be at least ¼″ deep.

7. Cut ⅛″ diameter dowels 3″ long and, with the finishing sander, make a point on one end. Using wood glue, secure the bills in the drilled holes with the point end out.

8. Using the finishing sander, prepare all surfaces for finishing. Also sand the bases, to enhance their appearance.

9. Use the many different-colored paints and small brushes that are available to paint the birds. You don't have to paint the support dowels or the bases.

Illus. 178. Covey of birds.

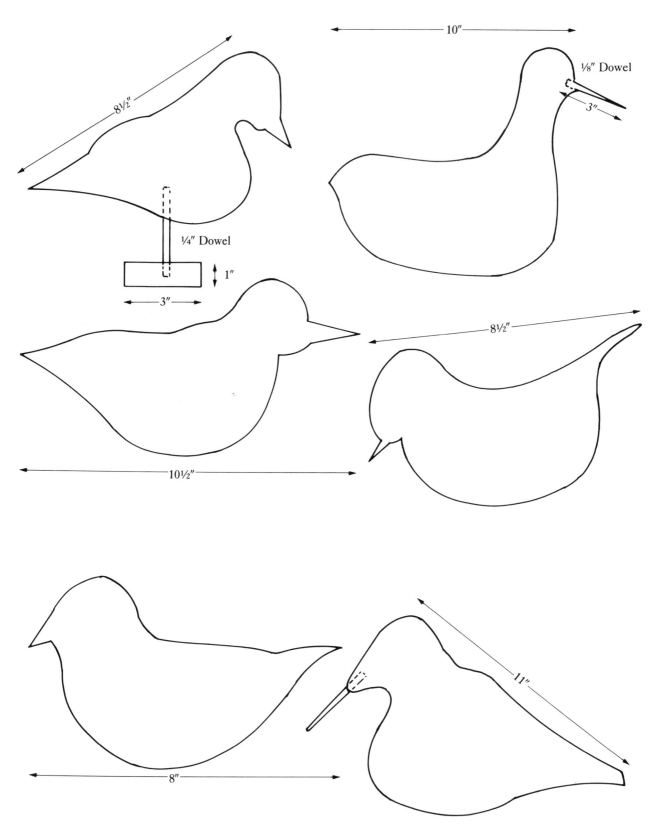

Illus. 179. Drawing of covey of birds.

69: *Shaker Peg Shelf*

(Illus. 180 and 181)

Named after the pegs developed by the early American religious community, this shelf is both functional and attractive. Though it is large enough to be used in any room of the house, you may want to modify its dimensions so that it will fit a particular spot. The Shaker pegs can be ordered from a mail-order supplier. The project looks good painted, and can be further enhanced with some stencil work. Incidentally, a plate groove can be routed on the top surface of the shelf.

MATERIAL:
- 1″ x 8″ pine
- Shaker pegs
- Finishing nails and wood glue
- Paint

TOOLS:
- Sabre or scroll saw
- Radial arm saw
- Table-mounted router with roundover bit
- Electric drill and ½″ bit
- Countersink drill
- Finishing sander

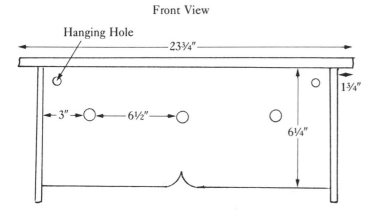

Illus. 180. Shaker peg shelf.

Front View

Hanging Hole

23¾″

1¾″

3″   6½″   6¼″

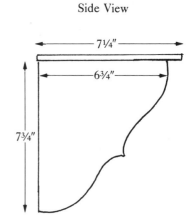

Side View

7¼″

6¾″

7¾″

Illus. 181. Drawing of Shaker peg shelf.

DIRECTIONS:

1. Measure and cut the shelf top. Refer to Illus. 181 for dimensions on all components.
2. Design, measure, and cut the back piece. The decorative portion can be done freehand.
3. Make a pattern for the legs from construction paper. Make the pattern to the suggested dimensions, trace it on a board, and cut it.
4. With a roundover bit, rout all edges that will not be attached to other edges.
5. Measure and mark the location of the Shaker pegs on the back piece. Using a ½″ diameter bit (if the Shaker pegs you are using have a ½″ diameter tenon), drill the holes where marked through the entire board.
6. Measure and drill, with the countersink, the hanging holes in the back piece.
7. Prepare all surfaces for finishing with the sander and a series of abrasive papers of varying grits. Wipe off the dust.
8. Spread wood glue in the peg holes, and on the pegs' tenons (just a little), then tap them in place. Put a piece of scrap between the peg and the hammer to avoid damaging them. If you have a wood mallet, use it.
9. Using wood glue and finishing nails, assemble the two legs to the back piece.
10. Spread glue on the top edges of the legs and the back piece and, with finishing nails, secure the shelf top to them. Make sure that there is equal distance on both ends between the ends of the shelf and the legs.
11. With a nail set, drive the heads of all nails under the surface of the wood.
12. Paint and decorate the shelf.

70: Fish Cutting Board

(Illus. 182 and 183)

As you will note from Illus. 182, this board is made from a very different-looking and attractive piece of hard rock maple. The eye of the fish is used to hang the board. Mineral oil is a good product to use for finishing the cutting board.

MATERIAL:
- 1″ (4/4's) thick hard rock maple
- Mineral oil

TOOLS:
- Sabre, scroll, or band saw
- Table-mounted router with roundover bit
- Drill press and 1¼″ multi-spur bit
- Finishing sander

DIRECTIONS:

1. Refer to Illus. 183 for the dimensions, and Illus. 182 for design ideas. You may want to make a pattern of the fish. If not, draw the design, freehand, on the maple board. Use a piece of maple that is distinctive and attractive. Cut out the fish as traced.
2. Cut a smiling mouth into the fish.
3. Drill the eye hole in the fish.
4. Using the roundover bit, rout all edges of the fish and both sides of the eye.
5. Prepare the surface and edges for finishing using various abrasive papers and a sander. Wipe off the dust.

Illus. 182. Fish cutting board.

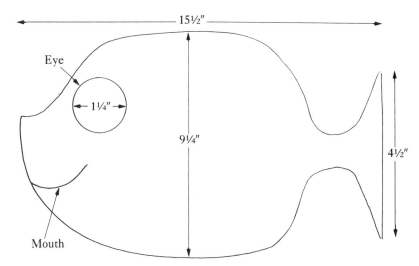

15½"

Eye

1¼"

9¼"

4½"

Mouth

Illus. 183. Drawing of fish cutting board.

6. Apply and rub mineral oil on the fish. If the oil or wood is warm, the oil will be absorbed more deeply and quickly. Allow the oil to dry.

71: *Clipboard 1* (Illus. 184

and 185)

Students, salespeople, and people in many other jobs will find the clipboard to be useful. This clipboard, made from pine, is enhanced with two strips of green veneer. While smaller than some clipboards, this one has ample room for scratch or narrow writing pads. The brass clip is available at craft stores and from mail-order suppliers. Very often, the suppliers have a variety of clips that are available. Veneer, if not available at a local hardwood dealer, can be ordered from mail-order suppliers.

MATERIAL:
• 1" x 8" pine
• ¹⁄₃₂" thick green veneer
• Brass clip
• Wood glue
• Clear lacquer

TOOLS:
• Sabre saw

• Radial arm saw
• Clamps
• Table-mounted router and roundover bit
• Scissors

DIRECTIONS:
1. Measure and cut the board to length.
2. Draw lines, as suggested in Illus. 185, where the veneer will be placed. Cut the board in sections along the lines.

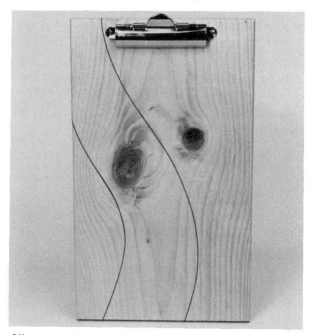

Illus. 184. Clipboard 1.

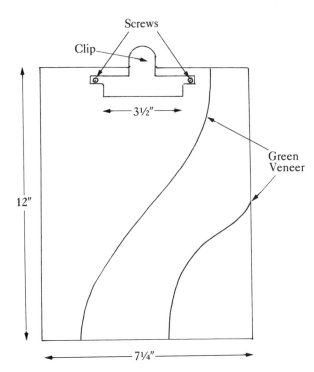

Illus. 185. Drawing of clipboard 1.

Screws

Clip

3½″

12″

Green Veneer

7¼″

3. Cut strips of veneer. Make them long enough to fit between the cut sections. The veneer should also be about ¼″ wider than the board.
4. Spread wood glue on all the edges of the cut sections of the board. Place the veneer between the sections and clamp them together. You may have to realign and reclamp the various sections and the veneer if they slide from the glue. Allow the glue to dry.
5. Using coarse-grit abrasive paper, sand away any excess glue and veneer.

6. Rout all the edges with the roundover bit.
7. Prepare the surfaces for finishing using fine-grit abrasive paper and a sander.
8. Finish the board with a clear lacquer. Apply several coats. Rub the board with steel wool (0000) between coats. Wax the surfaces with paste wax, and polish them.
9. Screw the clip to the board. Screws generally are provided with the clip.

72: *Coasters* (Illus. 186 and 187)

Every household needs coasters, and these black walnut coasters are especially appealing. Cork coaster discs can be ordered from mail-order catalogues or often can be found in local craft stores. You may want to use another hardwood that will better match the furniture the coasters will be placed on. A clear-lacquer or oil finish should be used.

MATERIAL:
• ¾″ (3/4's) thick black walnut
• Cork coaster discs
• Wood glue
• Oil or clear lacquer

TOOLS:
• Wood lathe and turning tools
• Band saw and ¼″ blade
• School compass
• Vernier caliper

Illus. 186. Coasters.

122

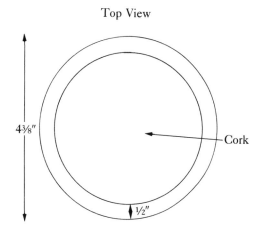

Top View

4⅜"

Cork

½"

Side View

⅛"

¾"

Cork

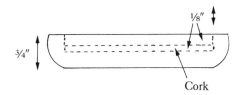

Illus. 187. Drawing of coaster.

DIRECTIONS:

1. Using the school compass, trace a number of round turning blocks. Cut the blocks using the band saw.
2. From pine scrap, cut glue blocks. Glue and clamp the pine pieces to the turning blocks.
3. Attach a faceplate to the glue block assembly and mount the assembly on the lathe. Check Illus. 187 prior to turning the assembly.
4. Turn the outside of the coaster with a ½" roundnose scraper. Turn the inside of the coaster with a 1" square-nose scraper.
5. Set the vernier caliper to the diameter of the cork discs. Use this setting to determine the inside diameter of the coaster. The cork has to fit neatly inside the coaster. The square-nose scraper is a good tool to use for this kind of task.
6. Separate the turned coaster from the glue block with the band saw. Sand the bottom surface of the coaster.
7. Finish the coaster with either clear lacquer or

oil. Do not put any finish on the surface where the cork disc will be glued. Allow the finish to dry.
8. Spread a thin film of glue on the inside coaster surface and set the cork disc in place. Clamp the disc until the glue is dry. Place a piece of scrap on the cork while clamping it.

73: Wine Rack

(Illus. 188 and 189)

A small wine rack makes an excellent house-warming gift. While this project is designed to hold three bottles of wine, it can easily be expanded to hold more. If you prefer, ⅜" diameter dowels can be used to stack several racks on top of one another. This wine rack is designed so that the bottles tip slightly forward, to ensure that wet corks are properly maintained. The rack can be painted and, if desired, decorated on its side surfaces.

MATERIAL:
- 1" x 4" pine
- Finishing nails and wood glue
- Paint

TOOLS:
- Sabre or scroll saw
- Radial arm saw or table saw
- Table-mounted router and roundover bit
- Finishing sander

DIRECTIONS:

1. Measure and cut the two side pieces. Refer to Illus. 189 for dimensions.
2. Measure and cut the front and back pieces to their required length and width.
3. Make patterns for the rounded areas on both the front and back pieces, trace them onto the wood, and cut them out.
4. Rout all the edges using a roundover bit. Do not rout the end edges of the front and back pieces.
5. Using wood glue and finishing nails, assemble

Illus. 188. Wine rack.

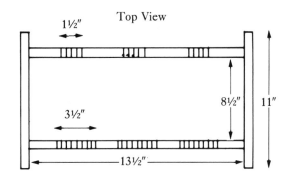

Top View

1½″

8½″   11″

3½″

13½″

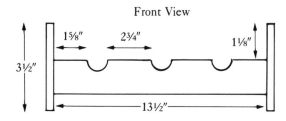

Front View

1⅝″   2¾″   1⅛″

3½″

13½″

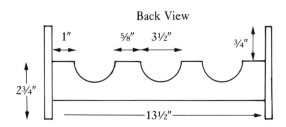

Back View

1″   ⅝″   3½″   ¾″

2¾″

13½″

Illus. 189. Drawing of wine rack.

the side pieces to the front and back pieces. Refer to Illus. 189 for proper placement of the front and back pieces.

6. Prepare the surfaces for finishing, and wipe off the dust.

7. Paint or decorate as desired.

74: Sleigh Christmas-Card Holder (Illus. 190 and 191)

This is an ideal way to keep Christmas cards in one place, yet still make them available for everyone to read and enjoy. The sleigh shown in Illus. 190 is painted red with black runners. You may prefer to mix in some green or some other seasonal decorations on the sides of the sleigh. Small blocks of wood are placed on the bottom to keep the cards standing upright.

MATERIAL:
- ⅜″ thick plywood
- ¼″ square scraps of pine
- Wood glue and wire brads
- Paint and wood putty

TOOLS:
- Sabre or scroll saw
- Finishing sander

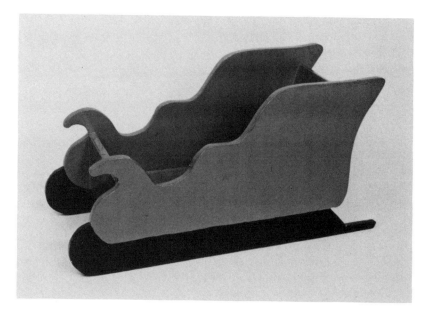

Illus. 190. *Sleigh Christmas-card holder.*

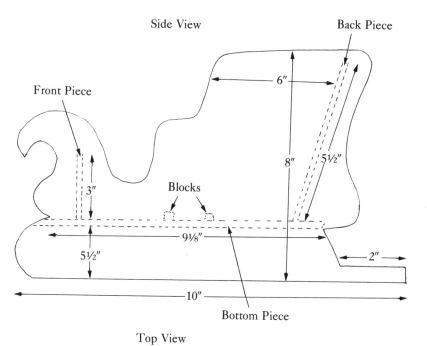

Side View

Back Piece

Front Piece

6"

8"   5½"

Blocks

3"

9⅛"

5½"

2"

10"

Bottom Piece

Illus. 191. *Drawing of sleigh Christmas-card holder.*

Top View

9⅛"

Blocks to Hold Up Card

6"

125

DIRECTIONS:

1. Tape two pieces of standard construction paper together and make a pattern of the sleigh's side piece. Refer to Illus. 191 for both dimensions and ideas on design.
2. Trace the pattern onto the surface of the plywood and cut it. Remember, you need two sides.
3. Measure and cut the back, front, and bottom pieces of the sleigh. Illus. 191 provides specific dimensions for these parts.
4. Using wood glue and brads, attach the front and bottom pieces.
5. Attach the two side pieces to the front and bottom pieces.
6. Place the back piece at an angle and secure it to both sides and the bottom piece. Illus. 191 will assist you in this placement.
7. Allow the glue to dry.
8. Cut and secure small pine blocks to the bottom surface.
9. Fill any holes in the edges of the plywood with wood putty.
10. Sand the edges and surfaces in preparation for painting. Wipe off the dust.
11. Paint and decorate as desired.

75: Fire-Starter Match Holder (Illus. 192 and 193)

This very different type of match holder can be used to light candles, light a fireplace, or for any number of other tasks. The holder requires wooden matches. The match is held in the ³⁄₁₆″ tubing and, when it goes out, the ⅛″ tubing forces it from the larger tubing. The holders can be turned from scrap hardwood and made in a variety of lengths. They are an ideal project for the spindle turner. Use a piece of buckskin to hang a long holder.

MATERIAL:

- ¾″ (3/4's) thick hardwood
- ⅛″, ³⁄₁₆″, and ½″ diameter brass tubing
- Clear lacquer

TOOLS:

- Wood lathe and turning tools
- Hacksaw
- Vernier caliper
- Chuck
- Drill press and ⅛″ (aircraft) and ³⁄₁₆″ diameter bits

DIRECTIONS:

1. Cut a series of turning spindles to the desired lengths from scrap hardwood. One short spindle and one longer spindle are used for this holder. Refer to Illus. 193 for details.
2. Mark the center of the long spindle and drill a ³⁄₁₆″ diameter hole approximately 1″ deep. At the center of the other end of the long spindle, drill a ⅛″ diameter hole the full length of the spindle until it joins the ³⁄₁₆″ hole. Thus, you will have a drilled hole through the entire spindle. If you have a chuck, secure the bits in the tailstock and drill the holes on the lathe. If not, use a drill press.
3. Drill a ⅛″ diameter hole approximately ½″ deep at the center of one end of the short spindle.
4. Secure the short spindle to the lathe, centering it at the drilled hole. Turn the spindle as desired, but in such a way that it will appear to be one piece when aligned with the larger spindle. Refer to the Illus. 193 and 194.
5. Turn the larger spindle to shape a ½″ diameter, ½″ long tenon on its bottom end. A vernier caliper will help you with this task. Make sure that you center the spindle around the drilled holes. Again, the top should align neatly with the bottom end of the short spindle. When assembled, the two turned pieces should look like one handle.
6. Measure and cut, with a hacksaw, a ½″ diameter brass ring that will fit tightly over the tenon. (Brass tubing and similar materials are usually available at a local hardware store.) Slip the ring over the tenon. Using a sander, make the two flush.
7. With the hacksaw, cut a 2⅝″ long piece of ³⁄₁₆″ diameter brass tubing. Carefully tap the tubing into the tenon hole. Let approximately 1⅝″ of the tubing extend beyond the tenon.

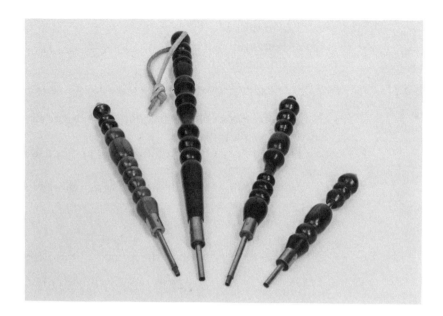

Illus. 192. Fire-starter match holders.

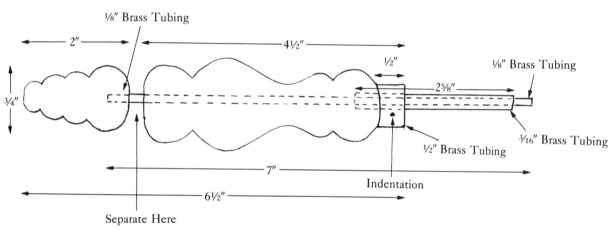

Illus. 193. Drawing of fire-starter match holder.

8. Punch two small indentations in the side of the brass tenon ring. This can be done with a nail. These indentations will prevent the ring from slipping off the tenon.

9. Measure and cut, with a hacksaw, a piece of ⅛″ diameter tubing that will extend from the top piece, through the bottom piece, and into the protruding section of 3/16″ tubing. Make sure that it slides easily through the bottom piece and the 3/16″ tubing.

10. Spread glue in the drilled ⅛″ diameter hole in the top piece and tap the ⅛″ tubing into it. Allow the glue to dry.

11. Slide the ⅛″ tubing all the way through the

bottom section and the protruding 3/16″ piece. The ⅛″ tubing should extend at least ⅛″ beyond the end of the 3/16″ tubing. You may have to saw off some excess tubing.

12. Pull the top piece and the ⅛″ tubing back about 1″ from the bottom piece. Slip part of a wooden match, approximately ⅜″ of it, into the 3/16″ tubing. Light the match. After blowing out the match, push the top piece and the ⅛″ tubing down to force out the used match.

13. Finish the holder with clear lacquer. Be careful not to get lacquer on the brass tubing. If the tubing tends to stick, rub it with steel wool (0000).

127

76: *Shaker Coat/Robe Hanger* (Illus. 194 and 195)

This functional and decorative Shaker hanger is easy to craft and makes an unusual gift. You may want to make one and hang it on a Shaker peg in a hallway. (A buckskin lace is used for hanging.) Stain and paint a decoration on those hangers that will serve as gifts.

MATERIAL:
- 1″ x 4″ pine
- Buckskin lace
- Stain and lacquer

TOOLS:
- Scroll or sabre saw
- Electric drill and ¼″ bit
- Table-mounted router and roundover bit
- Finishing sander

DIRECTIONS:
1. Join two pieces of construction paper together and make a pattern of the hanger.
2. Trace the pattern on a pine board and cut it. You may want to make several.
3. Center, mark, and drill the two hanging holes. They should be at least ¼″ in diameter, in order to accommodate a buckskin lace.
4. Rout all edges with the roundover bit.
5. With a sander, prepare the project for finishing. Wipe off all dust.
6. Stain and lacquer the project. Paint decorations, and then thread a piece of buckskin through the holes for hanging.

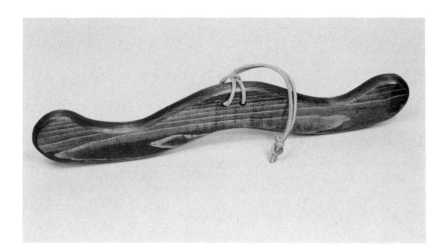

Illus. 194. Shaker coat/robe hanger.

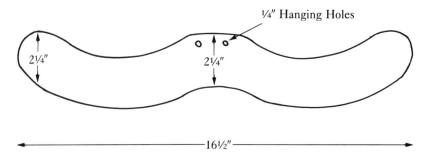

Illus. 195. Drawing of Shaker coat/robe hanger.

¼″ Hanging Holes

2¼″

2¼″

16½″

77: *Shorebird 5* (Illus. 196

and 197)

The bill and the turn of the head on this shore-bird will present you with a bit of a challenge, but it's well worth the effort. To assist you in making the project, refer to Gift Project 4.

MATERIAL:
- 2½″ (10/4's) thick basswood
- ¼″ dowel
- ⅛″ dowel
- Slice of log
- Lacquer

TOOLS:
- Band saw and ¼″ blade
- Electric grinder
- Large tungsten carbide burrs
- Carving or sloyd knife
- Electric drill and bits (⅛″ and ¼″)
- Finishing sander

DIRECTIONS:
1. Prepare a rough block of the bird based on Illus. 196 and 197. The dimensions given are all finished dimensions, so use a bit more wood. Remove as much excess wood as possible with the band saw.
2. Remove wood and shape the bird using the various suggested tools.
3. Use a finishing sander for the final shaping and surface preparation. Use a variety of abrasive grits ranging from coarse to extra-fine.
4. Measure, design, and cut the bill for the bird from a piece of scrap. Shape the bill and prepare it for finishing.
5. Dill a ⅛″ diameter hole into the bill and one into the head of the bird where the bill will be attached.
6. Cut a 1″ long piece of ⅛″ diameter dowel. Spread glue on the dowel and the back surface of the bill. Place the dowel into the drilled hole in the head. Allow the glue to dry.
7. Drill a ¼″ diameter hole in the bottom center

Illus. 196. Shorebird 5.

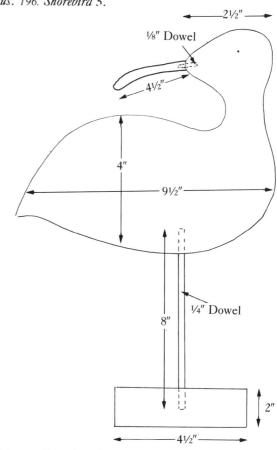

Illus. 197. Drawing of shorebird 5.

of the body for the support dowel. Cut a 9″ long piece of ¼″ dowel.

8. Using a band saw, cut a 4½″ diameter slice of log that is about 2″ thick. Drill a ¼″ diameter hole into the top center of the slice.

9. Place one end of the ¼″ dowel into the bird and the other into the support base.

10. Locate the placement of the eyes. With a small nail or punch, make an eye indentation on each side of the head.

11. Finish the bird with a clear lacquer, rubbing the finish with steel wool (0000) between coats. A final rubbing with paste wax makes for an excellent finish.

78: *Basket Box*

(Illus. 198 and 199)

A wooden box that can function as a basket makes an ideal gift. The box presented here can be used as a garden/yard box or to hold and display gourds and other dried items. You can also paint or stencil some decorations on the box.

MATERIAL:
- ½″ x 6″ pine
- ½″ x 4″ pine
- Finishing nails and wood glue
- Paint

TOOLS:
- Sabre or scroll saw
- Table or radial arm saw
- Band saw and ½″ blade
- Table-mounted router and roundover bit
- Electric drill and ½″ bit
- Finishing sander

DIRECTIONS:
1. Measure and design an end piece on the surface of a ½″ x 6″ board. Saw it out and use it as a pattern for the second needed end piece. If you don't have ½″ thick stock, rip it on a band saw using a ½″ wide blade.

2. Draw the finger holes on the side pieces using the suggested dimensions. Drill a hole inside and through the area, thread a sabre-saw blade through the hole, and cut the finger holes.

3. Measure and cut the two side pieces. Refer to Illus. 199 for dimensions.

4. Rout the edges with a roundover bit.

5. Using wood glue and finishing nails, attach the side pieces to the end pieces.

6. With a finishing sander and coarse-grit abrasive paper, sand the bottom edges of the side pieces to match the angle of the end pieces.

7. Measure and cut sufficient pieces to cover the bottom of the box.

8. Nail and glue the bottom pieces to the sides and ends. Using a nail set, drive the heads of all the nails under the wood's surface.

9. With the finishing sander, prepare the surfaces for painting. Also, sand the edges in such a way so that they appear worn or used.

10. Paint and decorate the basket box. Grey paint looks good.

Illus. 198. Basket box.

Side View

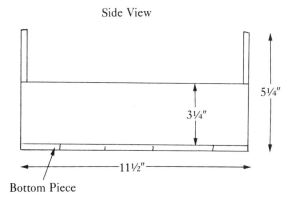

5¼"

3¼"

11½"

Bottom Piece

End View

Finger Hole

4½"

1¼"

10¾"

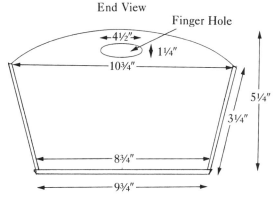

5¼"

3¼"

8¾"

9¾"

Illus. 199. Drawing of basket box.

79: Round Mirrors (Illus. 200 and 201)

Mirrors of any size or design make a fine gift. When they're round, off-set, and painted, they will get even more attention and appreciation. If you're so inclined, there is sufficient surface to add some decoration to the frame.

MATERIAL:
• 1″ x 10″ pine
• Mirror
• White glue and construction paper
• Paint
• Sawtooth hanger

TOOLS:
• Sabre saw
• School compass
• Circle glass cutter
• Table-mounted router with rabbeting and roundover bits
• Circle cutter and drill press
• Finishing sander

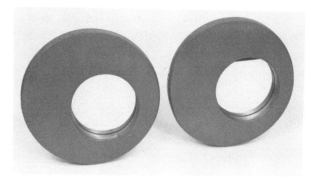

Illus. 200. Round mirrors.

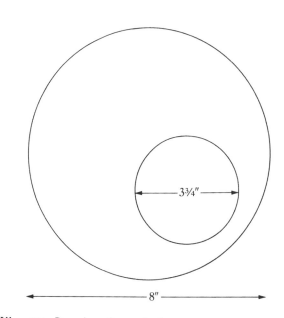

3¾"

8″

Illus. 201. Drawing of round mirrors.

DIRECTIONS:
1. With a school compass, make an 8″ diameter circle on a board. You may want to make several of these mirrors, of different diameters. Cut the frames along the line made by the compass using a sabre saw. Take your time and follow the line.
2. Decide where on the frame you want the mirror to be, and make another circle with the school compass. Illus. 201 suggests a 3¾″ diameter cir-

cle. If you have a drill press and a circle cutter, set the cutter and make the hole. If not, drill a ½" diameter hole inside the circle, thread a sabre-saw blade through the hole, and cut out the circle.

3. On the back edge of the mirror area, rout a rabbet that is at least ⅛" deep. This routed area will accommodate the round piece of mirror.

4. Using a roundover bit, rout all edges on the frame and also the front edge of the mirror area.

5. Go over all surfaces with the finishing sander. Wipe off the dust. Paint and decorate the frame.

6. Measure the diameter of the inside rabbeted area. Using a circle glass cutter, either cut a piece of mirror to the needed diameter yourself or have the local glass shop do it. You don't need expensive mirror glass for this project.

7. Spread a small bead of glue inside the rabbeted area and set the mirror in place. Don't use too much glue, as you do not want it to squeeze out on the front surface of the mirror. Allow the glue to dry.

8. Cut a round piece of construction paper and glue it to the back of the frame. This will cover the mirror area and make the whole project look neater.

9. Center and secure a sawtooth or other hanger to the back of the frame. When using the hammer, be careful that you don't break the mirror.

80: Children's Book Holder (Illus. 202 and 203)

This book holder is the kind of item that will be sought by adults as well as children. A pair of green giraffes with white polka dots slide back and forth on two pieces of ¾" dowels.

MATERIAL:
- 1" x 6" pine
- ¾" diameter dowels
- Paint

TOOLS:
- Sabre or scroll saw
- Electric drill and ¾" bit
- Table-mounted router with roundover bit
- Finishing sander
- Round rasp

DIRECTIONS:
1. With a piece of construction paper, make a pattern using Illus. 203 and 204 as guides.

2. Trace the pattern on a pine board and cut it. Remember, you need two giraffes.

3. Measure, mark, and drill two ¾" diameter holes in each giraffe. Make sure the holes are drilled at the same locations on both giraffes.

4. Rout all edges with a roundover bit.

5. Cut two pieces of ¾" diameter dowel approximately 12" long. If you want the holder to accommodate more books, make the dowels longer.

6. With the finishing sander, round over the edges of the dowels. Test the dowels in the drilled holes for fit. If they're too tight, widen the holes, carefully, with the round rasp. If available, use a Moto Tool with a sanding sleeve instead.

7. Prepare all surfaces for painting. Wipe off the dust.

Illus. 202. Children's book holder.

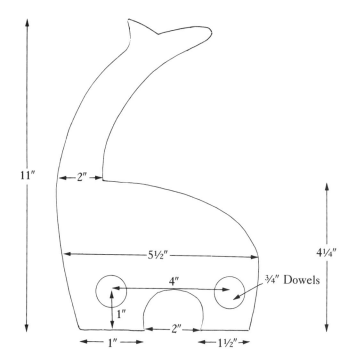

11″
2″
5½″
4¼″
4″   ¾″ Dowels
1″
2″
1″   1½″

8. Paint and decorate the giraffes. Use unusual bold colors. Avoid getting any paint in the dowel holes. Make sure that the paint is dry before inserting the dowels through the drilled holes.

81: Marble/Maple Cutting and Serving Piece (Illus. 204 and 205)

A hard-rock maple cutting board with a round piece of marble secured to it makes an attractive serving piece. It is very useful for cutting and serving cheese and sausage or other goodies. If you're so inclined, make a round or different-shaped cutting board to secure the marble. The marble can be ordered from several mail-order suppliers.

MATERIAL:
• 1″ (4/4's) thick hard maple
• 6″ diameter marble tile
• Waterproof glue
• Mineral oil

TOOLS:
• Sabre or band saw
• Table-mounted router with roundover bit
• Finishing sander

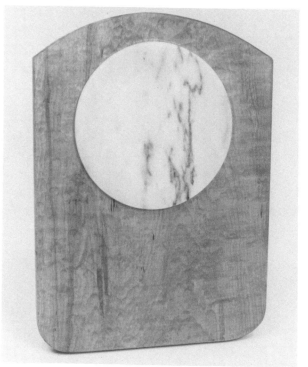

Illus. 204. Marble/maple cutting and service piece.

133

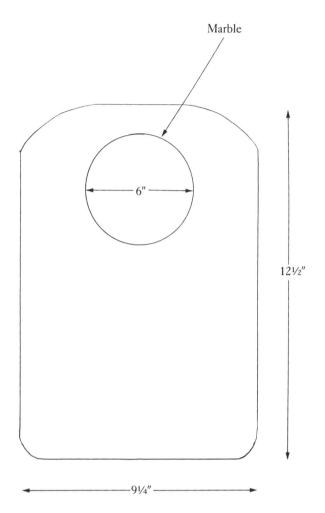

Marble

6"

12½"

9¼"

Illus. 205. Drawing of marble/maple cutting and servicing piece.

82: *Turned Table Lamp*

(Illus. 206 and 207)

For those with a lathe, table lamps are fun to make and to give as gifts. This lamp is turned from black walnut and is finished with a clear lacquer. You may want to use less expensive hardwood, or a less thick wood. The various electrical components for a lamp can be purchased separately or as a kit from a local discount or hardware store. Some mail-order suppliers can also provide all the parts. Any information needed to wire a socket or plug is generally given on the back of the part's package. No special tools are required for assembly.

Illus. 206. Turned table lamp.

DIRECTIONS:

1. Measure, design, and cut the board. While you may want to duplicate the project design, you should also, at least, consider a different shape.

2. Rout the edges of the board with a round-over bit.

3. Prepare the surfaces for finishing. Wipe off the dust.

4. Locate and glue the marble tile to the board. While white glue will hold the tile in place, frequent washing may break the glue bond. Waterproof glue would be a better choice.

5. Oil the board with mineral oil. Do not get any oil on the marble tile.

134

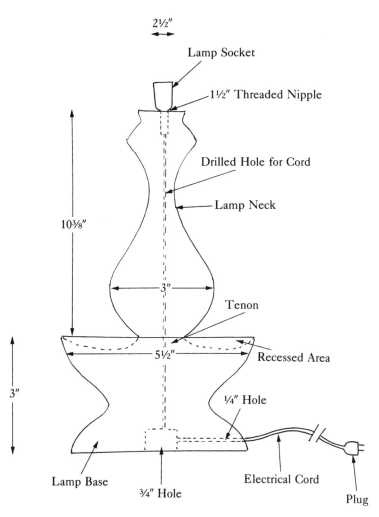

Illus. 207. *Drawing of turned table lamp.*

MATERIAL:

- 3″ (12/4's) thick black walnut
- Lamp socket
- 1½″ threaded nipple (2)
- 6′ lamp cord and plug
- Lacquer

TOOLS:

- Wood lathe and turning tools
- Band saw and ¼″ blade
- Chuck
- Drill press and 5/16″ long, ¼″ (aircraft) and ¾″ diameter bits
- Finishing sander
- Vernier caliper

DIRECTIONS:

1. Measure and cut a spindle for the lamp neck. Refer to Illus. 206 and 207 for design ideas and dimensions.

2. Using a four-prong drive and a revolving center, turn the lamp neck to its shape.

3. At the center mark made by the revolving center, drill a 5/16″ diameter hole through the entire piece. Use a drill to ensure straightness of the hole.

4. Measure and cut a turning block for the lamp base. If you do not have a commercial chuck, use a glue block and faceplate to turn the base.

5. Turn the lamp base to its shape. Note in Illus. 207 that the tenon at the top center of the base will be joined to the bottom of the lamp neck. Use a vernier caliper to ensure that the tenon diameter is the same as the diameter of the lamp neck base. A recessed area should be turned between the tenon and the top edge of the base. Before removing the base from the lathe, make an indentation on the top surface of the tenon. Sand the base.

6. Drill a 5/16″ diameter hole, starting at the indentation and going through the base. In the bottom of the base, drill a 3/4″ diameter hole into the 5/16″ hole. The 3/4″ hole should be at least 1″ deep.

7. In the side of the base, approximately 1/4″ up from the bottom surface, drill a 1/4″ diameter hole that extends into the 3/4″ hole. Refer to Illus. 207. The lamp cord will eventually pass through all these holes and out the side of the base.

8. Use a mallet or a piece of scrap and a hammer to tap a threaded nipple into the 5/16″ hole at the top of the lamp neck. Approximately 3/8″ of the nipple should extend above the top surface of the neck. Be careful that you do not damage the threads on the nipple.

9. Thread the lamp cord through the nipple and down through the entire length of the lamp neck. Tie a knot in the last 6″ of the lamp cord so that it cannot be pulled through. This will give you more than enough wire to connect to the lamp socket.

10. Tap a threaded nipple into the 5/16″ hole at the top of the lamp base. At least one-half of the nipple should extend out of the hole.

11. Thread the lamp cord through the nipple and to the bottom of the lamp base. Then thread it through the 1/4″ hole and out through the side of the base.

12. Spread wood glue on the top surface of the base tenon and the bottom surface of the lamp neck. Force the nipple into the hole in the bottom of the lamp neck. The two surfaces need to make contact. Allow the glue to dry. The brass nipple makes the joint between the two parts stronger.

13. Wire and attach the lamp socket to the top nipple. Secure the plug to the other end of the cord. Pull any excess cord through the lamp *after* the socket has been wired.

14. Place a bulb in the socket, plug in the wall outlet, and test the lamp.

15. Finish the lamp with a clear lacquer. Go over each coat with steel wool (0000). Be sure to wipe away the dust and steel hairs left by the wool. A final coat of paste wax will give the lamp a hard finish.

16. If you want, cut a round piece of felt and glue it to the bottom surface. This will prevent any possible scratching by the lamp of a table's surface.

17. Find a lampshade that's the right size and color and put it on the lamp.

83: *Clipboard 2* (Illus. 208 and 209)

A clipboard that will accommodate legal-size paper or pads makes a practical gift. One that's made from a highly figured piece of black walnut is especially appealing. As indicated with the earlier clipboard project, the metal clip can be ordered from mail-order suppliers.

MATERIAL:
- 1″ (4/4's) thick black walnut
- Clipboard clip
- Lacquer

TOOLS:
- Radial arm, table, or sabre saw
- Table-mounted router with roundover bit
- Finishing sander
- Electric drill and 1/32″ bit

DIRECTIONS:
1. Measure and cut the hardwood board. You may prefer using a wood other than walnut. Find a piece that has interesting color and grain.
2. Rout the edges of the board with the roundover bit.
3. Prepare the edges and surfaces for finishing.
4. Apply a clear-lacquer finish. Rub between

Illus. 208. Clipboard 2.

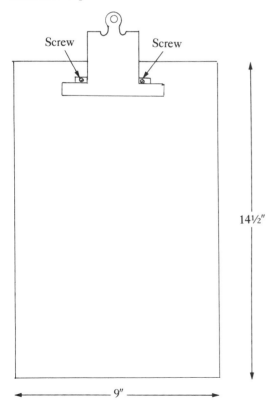

Screw   Screw

14½"

9"

Illus. 209. Drawing of clipboard 2.

coats with steel wool (0000). Paste wax should be applied as a final coat.

5. Align and center the clip near the top edge of the board. Mark the screw holes on the surface.

6. Drill small pilot holes for the screws. This will prevent the screws from cracking the wood. It will also make them easier to screw into the wood.

7. Secure the clip to the board with the provided screws.

84: *Geese Decoys* (Illus. 210 and 211)

For the person who is fond of geese or wants something different for his yard, these decoys will be a highly prized gift. Made life-size and painted to resemble a Canadian goose, they are effective decoys. Make the project from outside plywood and use exterior paints.

MATERIAL:
- ¼" outside plywood
- ¾" dowels
- ⅛" bolts and nuts
- Poster board
- Grey, black, and white exterior paints

TOOLS:
- Sabre, scroll, or band saw
- Electric drill and ⅛" bit
- Finishing sander

DIRECTIONS:
1. Make a pattern for each pose using a large sheet of poster board. Design and draw the two decoys carefully. The better the patterns, the more life-like the geese.

2. Trace the patterns on the surface of outdoor-grade plywood. Cut the birds as traced.

3. Measure and cut two ¾" diameter dowels 12" long.

4. Cut a groove in the top of each dowel that is ¼" wide and 2" deep. Refer to Illus. 211.

Illus. 210. Goose decoy.

Illus. 211. Drawing of goose decoy.

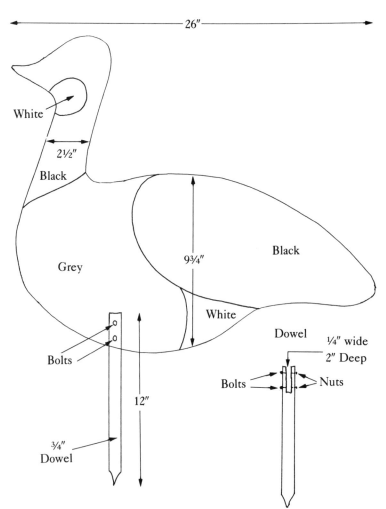

26″

White

2½″

Black

9¾″

Black

Grey

White

Dowel

¼″ wide

2″ Deep

Bolts

Nuts

Bolts

12″

¾″
Dowel

5. Drill two ⅛″ diameter holes through each dowel and groove. Bolts will penetrate these holes for securing the dowel to the goose.

6. Sharpen the other end of the dowel so that the goose can be pushed easily into the ground.

7. Slide the dowel groove over the bottom center of a bird. While holding it straight, drill a ⅛″ diameter hole through the previously drilled hole and through the goose. Insert a bolt and thread on a nut. Repeat the process with the second hole and the other goose. When all the bolts and nuts are in place, tighten them.

8. Refer to Illus. 210 and 211 to note how the geese are painted. Using a pencil, label the colors on areas where they will be used.

9. Paint the geese using the suggested colors. You will have to apply several coats or the geese will not hold up against the weather. Again, it's important to remember that these are but approximations of geese.

85: Strawberry Fish on Wheels (Illus. 212 and 213)

The strawberry fish on wheels is an excellent gift for that special child who would enjoy a colorful pull toy, or for that person who likes to display bright and colorful items. The project is great fun to make and even more fun to paint and decorate.

MATERIAL:
- 1″ x 10″ pine
- 1″ x 4″ pine
- 1¾″ wooden wheels and axles
- 2 eye screws
- Cord
- 1″ wooden ball
- Wood screws and wood glue
- Paints

TOOLS:
- Sabre or scroll saw
- Electric drill and ¼″ bit
- Finishing sander

DIRECTIONS:

1. Draw and cut a pattern of the fish. Refer to Illus. 212 and 213 for design ideas and dimensions.

2. Trace the pattern on a piece of pine and cut it.

3. Measure and cut the trailer from a piece of 1″ x 4″ pine.

4. Locate and mark the placement of the four wheels on the sides of the trailer. Drill ¼″ diameter holes at each location to hold the wheel axles.

5. Using wood glue and wood screws, secure the fish to the trailer. The screws should penetrate from the bottom of the trailer and into the fish. Allow the glue to dry.

6. Lightly sand all edges to remove any potential splinters or sharp corners.

7. Paint the fish, trailer, wheels, and axle hubs with the suggested paints or those you prefer. Also paint the wooden ball.

8. Place a spot of glue in the drilled axle holes and, with the wheels in place, tap the axles into the holes. Leave enough space between the wheels and trailer so that the wheels can move freely.

9. Thread an eye screw into the front center of the trailer and also into the wooden ball. Attach a length of cord to both eye screws; this cord is used to pull the toy.

Illus. 212. Strawberry fish on wheels.

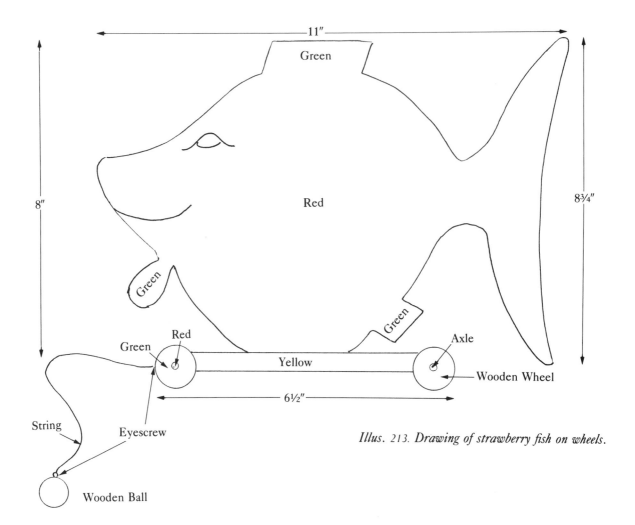

11″

Green

Red

Green

Green

8″

8¾″

Green

Red

Axle

Yellow

Wooden Wheel

6½″

String

Eyescrew

Wooden Ball

Illus. 213. Drawing of strawberry fish on wheels.

86: Collector's Shelf (Illus. 214 and 215)

This Early American shelf is an excellent one on which to display small collectibles. It is large enough for a sizeable collection, yet will not overwhelm a wall. The shelf looks best painted. Its color should match the collection or the wall on which it will be hung.

MATERIAL:
- ½″ x 10″ pine
- ³⁄₁₆″ x 4″ pine
- Finishing nails, wire brads, and wood glue
- Paint

TOOLS:
- Sabre, scroll, or band saw
- Radial arm or table saw
- Table-mounted router and ³⁄₁₆″ straight bit
- Electric drill
- Countersink drill
- Finishing sander

DIRECTIONS:
1. Study the design and dimensions as presented in Illus. 215. Measure, design, and cut the back piece from ½″ thick pine.
2. Measure and mark the hanging hole on the back piece. Drill the hole with a countersink drill.

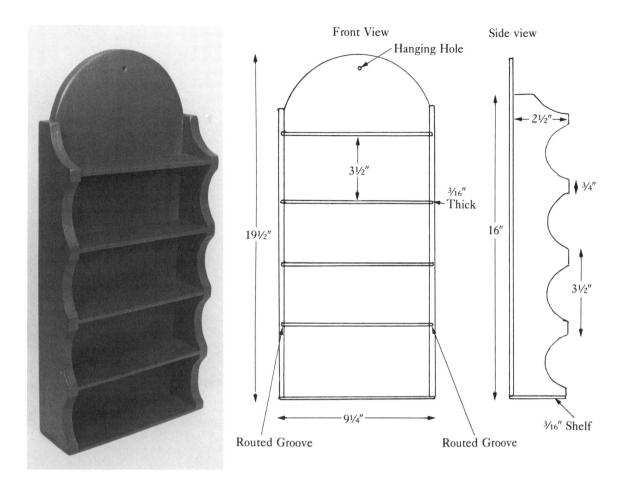

Front View   Side view

Hanging Hole

3½″

³⁄₁₆″ Thick

19½″

9¼″

Routed Groove   Routed Groove

2½″

¾″

16″

3½″

³⁄₁₆″ Shelf

Illus. 214. Collector's shelf.   *Illus. 215. Drawing of collector's shelf.*

3. Draw a side piece on a ½″ thick piece of 4″ wide pine. Refer to Illus. 215 for the various dimensions. Cut the side piece.

4. Using the first side piece as a pattern, trace and cut the second side piece.

5. Rout a ³⁄₁₆″ wide and ⅜″ deep groove into the inside surface of each side piece. The shelves are held in these grooves. Using a fence and adjusting it for each separate rout, make the grooves with a table-mounted router. Given the depth of cut needed, make two passes. Take your time with the routing tasks. The grooves should be straight and accurately placed in the side pieces.

6. With wood glue and finishing nails, attach the two side pieces to the back piece. The sides should be placed ³⁄₁₆″ above the bottom edge of

the back piece. This is to allow space for the shelf that will be attached here.

7. Measure and cut four shelves that are ³⁄₁₆″ thick. The fifth shelf, also ³⁄₁₆″ thick, is longer because it is secured to the bottom of the two side pieces.

8. Spread a bead of wood glue in the routed grooves and tap a shelf in place. There is no need to nail the shelves in place. After the four shelves are secure in their grooves, using wood glue and brads, attach the fifth shelf to the bottom ends of the two side pieces. Allow the glue to dry.

9. Lightly sand all edges with a finishing sander. Prepare all surfaces for finishing. Wipe off the dust.

10. Paint the shelf an appropriate color.

87: Paper-Clip Holder

(Illus. 216 and 217)

As a desktop piece, a turned paper-clip holder can be not only functional, but a conversation piece. Use a distinctive piece of wood. Perhaps you can find one in the scrap box. If not, search the hardwood dealer. You may even want to use one of the imports.

MATERIAL:

• 1½″ (6/4's) thick hardwood
• Lacquer

TOOLS:

• Wood lathe and turning tools
• Chuck
• Band saw
• School compass
• Finishing sander

DIRECTIONS:

1. Using the school compass, make an oversize turning block for the project. Cut the block using a band saw.

2. If you do not have a commercial chuck, make a round glue block with the compass from a piece of scrap pine. Cut the block and then glue and clamp it to the turning block. When the glue is dry, attach a faceplate and secure the turning block to the lathe.

3. Turn the holder to shape. A ½″ roundnose scraper will work well for turning the rounded inside of the holder. Make the inside deep enough to hold a supply of clips.

4. If a glue block is being used, turn or saw off the turned piece. Prepare the bottom surface for finishing using an electric sander.

5. If you want, before finishing, write a message and date on the bottom of the holder. Use an alcohol pen. Don't forget to put your logo on it as well.

6. Finish the holder with a clear lacquer. Between coats, rub the surface with steel wool (0000). A final coat of paste wax will complete the project.

Illus. 216. Paper-clip holder.

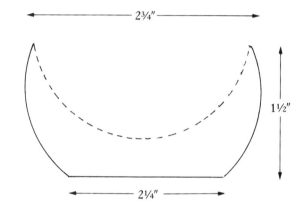

Illus. 217. Drawing of paper-clip holder.

88: Hanging Candle Holder (Illus. 218 and 219)

Hearts are a popular design concept, and a hanging candle holder shaped like a heart will make an appealing gift. Not only is the back of this holder shaped like a heart, so is the small shelf that supports the candle cup. The candle cups, available from mail-order suppliers, will hold a ⅝″ diameter candle base. If the size of this project is increased, larger candle cups should be used. The holders can be painted a bright red, and some decorative touches can be made.

MATERIAL:

• 1″ x 6″ pine
• Candle cups
• Wood glue and finishing nails

Illus. 218. Hanging candle holders.

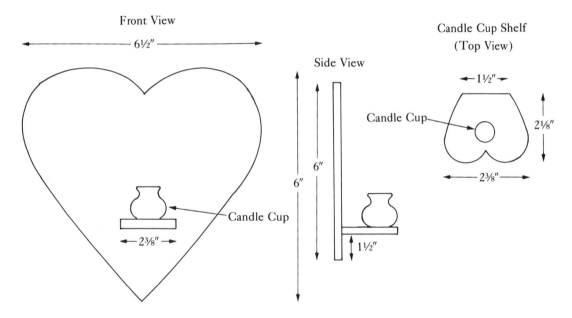

Front View

6½"

6"

2⅜"

Candle Cup

Side View

6"

6"

1½"

Candle Cup Shelf
(Top View)

1½"

Candle Cup

2⅛"

2⅜"

Illus. 219. Drawing of hanging candle holder.

- Sawtooth hangers
- Paint

TOOLS:
- Sabre or scroll saw
- Table-mounted router with roundover bit
- Finishing sander

DIRECTIONS:
1. Make a heart pattern from construction paper for the back piece of the holder. Refer to the suggested dimensions in Illus. 219.

2. Trace the heart pattern onto a pine board and cut it. Two back pieces have to be made.

3. With construction paper, make a pattern of the candle cup shelf. Trace the pattern on a piece of scrap material and cut it. Two cup shelves are also needed.

4. Rout all the edges of both the back piece and the cup shelf with a roundover bit. Do not rout the edges of the cup shelf that will attach to the back piece.

5. Center and glue the candle cups to the cup shelves. Drive a small finishing nail through the shelf and into the bottom of the cup. This and the glue should hold the cup firmly in place.

6. Measure and mark the location of the cup shelves on the front surface of the back piece. Glue and nail the shelves in place.

7. Using the finishing sander, prepare all surfaces and edges for painting. Wipe off the dust.

8. Paint and decorate the holders.

9. Secure sawtooth hangers to the backs of the holders.

89: *Bookmarks*

(Illus. 220 and 221)

Wooden bookmarks are a rarity and would be especially prized by someone who enjoys reading. They can be easily made by cutting a thin slice from either an imported wood or an attractive local hardwood. Wood-burn or paint a design on the bookmark, or simply display the wood with a clear oil or lacquer finish. If you have a planer or access to one, create bookmarks with a variety of designs and thicknesses. Remember to check the scrap box for wood.

MATERIAL:
• 1/16" thick hardwood
• Paint, oil, or lacquer

TOOLS:
• Band saw and 1/2" blade
• Planer
• Scroll saw
• Wood-burning tool
• Finishing sander

DIRECTIONS:
1. Plane hardwood or resaw it with the band saw to a thickness of 1/16". If the band saw leaves a rough surface, sand the surfaces smooth.

2. Design, measure, and cut a series of bookmarks. Refer to Illus. 221 for design ideas and dimensions, but also use your own.

3. If you have a wood-burning tool, try some designs on one or both surfaces.

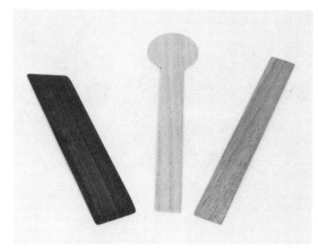

Illus. 220. Bookmarks.

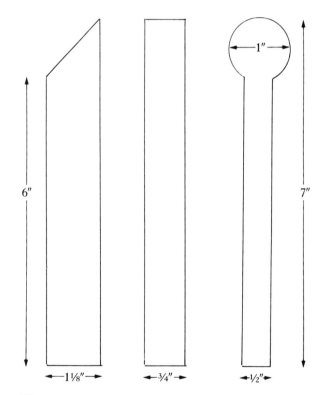

Illus. 221. Drawing of bookmarks.

4. Lightly sand the surfaces and edges in preparation for finishing. Remove the dust.

5. Apply oil, lacquer, or paint to the bookmarks. Do some decorative painting on them or stencil them.

90: Clock Shelf

(Illus. 222 and 223)

Although this project is traditionally called a clock shelf, it can be used to display any item. It is large and stable enough to hold and display something heavy, and can also be modified to meet a particular display need. Although this shelf is made from black walnut, another hardwood or pine can be used.

MATERIAL:
- ¾″ (3/4's) thick black walnut
- ½″ flattop walnut screw-hole plugs
- Wood screws and wood glue
- Oil or lacquer

TOOLS:
- Sabre, band, radial, or table saw
- Table-mounted router and roundover bit
- Electric drill and ½″ and ¹⁄₁₆″ bits
- Countersink drill
- Finishing sander

DIRECTIONS:
1. Measure and cut the shelf top. Refer to Illus. 222 for suggested dimensions.
2. Make a pattern of a leg from construction paper. Trace the pattern and cut two legs.
3. Measure and cut the support piece. Drill two hanging holes with the countersink drill.
4. Trace the ends of the support piece on the upper back surfaces of the legs. Refer to Illus. 223 for this location. Cut out this area on the inside of the traced lines. Check the fit of the support piece.
5. Rout the edges of the legs and the top piece. Don't rout edges that will join other parts. For example, don't rout the top edges of the legs.
6. Measure and mark the location of screws on the back of the support piece. These screws will secure the back piece to the cutout areas in the legs.
7. Using the countersink drill, make two screw holes in the back piece where marked.
8. With wood glue and screws, attach the back piece to the two legs. Allow the glue to dry.
9. Using the leg assembly as a guide, mark the location of the screw holes on the top surface of the shelf. Two screws should enter each leg from the top piece. Refer to Illus. 223 to note the distance between the side of each leg and the ends of the top piece.
10. Drill ½″ diameter holes at the four marked screw locations. The holes should be at least ⅜″ deep. At the center of each hole drill a ¹⁄₁₆″ diameter pilot hole through the piece.
11. Spread glue on the top edges of the legs and the support piece. Place the top piece on the assembly and screw it in place. Wipe off any glue that may have squeezed out onto the surfaces.
12. Put a touch of glue into each drilled hole and tap a flat screw plug in place. Allow the glue to dry.
13. Prepare the surface for finishing using an electric sander and abrasive papers of various grits.
14. Oil or lacquer the shelf.

Illus. 222. Clock shelf.

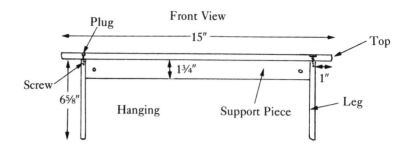

Front View

Plug · ────── 15″ ────── · Top

Screw   1¾″   1″

6⅝″   Hanging   Support Piece   Leg

Side View

Illus. 223. Drawing of clock shelf.

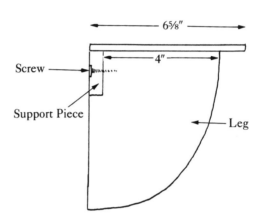

Screw ─────▶   ──── 6⅝″ ────
────── 4″ ──────

Support Piece   Leg

91: Scrap Mirrors (Illus. 224 and 225)

These small, decorative mirrors can be a useful and, when made from scrap, inexpensive gift. The only expense would be the brass-ring hangers or some other hanging device. While the project mirrors are stained and lacquered, you may want to consider painting and decorating them.

MATERIAL:
- Scraps of pine
- Scraps of mirror glass
- Ring hangers, mini brass hangers, or sawtooth hangers
- Construction paper
- White glue
- Stain and lacquer

TOOLS:
- Sabre, scroll, band, radial, or table saw
- Table-mounted router and rabbeting and round-over bits
- Electric drill and ¼″ bit
- School compass
- Standard and circle glass cutters
- Finishing sander

DIRECTIONS:
1. Using Illus. 225 and 226 as guides, draw patterns for a series of frames and cut them. Maximize your scraps. Try hardwood scraps if any are available. Develop your own designs. The patterns for some frames should be drawn on construction paper.

2. Draw and cut patterns for the frame mirror areas. Use a school compass or a template. An oval or round mirror can be difficult to draw freehand.

Illus. 224. Scrap mirrors.

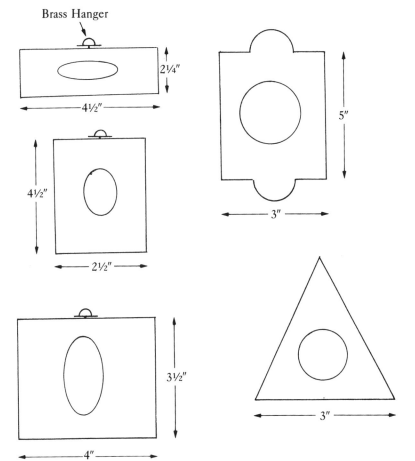

Brass Hanger

2¼"

4½"

4½"

2½"

5"

3"

Illus. 225. Drawing of scrap mirrors.

3½"

4"

3"

3. Center and trace the mirror area patterns on the frames. Drill a ¼" diameter hole inside the traced area, thread a sabre or scroll-saw blade through the pattern, and cut it.

4. With a rabbeting bit, rout the back of the mirror area. The rabbet should be approximately ⅛" deep in order to accommodate the glass.

5. Rout all edges with a roundover bit.

6. Prepare the surfaces and edges for finishing.

7. Stain and lacquer or paint the frames as desired.

8. Using either a standard or circle glass cutter, cut mirror glass to fit in the rabbeted area of the frames.

9. Spread a small bead of glue in the rabbeted area and set in the mirror glass. Press the mirror glue in place. Allow the glue to dry with the frame facing down.

10. Cut a piece of construction paper that will cover the back surface of the frame. Spread glue on the edges of the paper and apply it to the frame.

11. Clean the mirror and attach a hanger. You may want to write a message on the paper backing.

92: *Mushrooms on a Log* (Illus. 226 and 227)

For the mycologist or the collector of mushrooms, this may be the ideal gift. Utilizing a slice of log from the backyard and a few chunks of scrap pine, you can make an inexpensive and very attractive gift. If you spend enough time shaping the mushrooms, they will indeed look realistic. A clear lacquer finish on the project dresses it up and will preserve it. By the way, you may want to add a few very tiny mushrooms to the display on the log.

MATERIAL:
• 2″ x 4″ pine scraps
• 3″ to 4″ diameter log
• Wire brads
• Lacquer

TOOLS:
• Band saw
• Electric grinder
• Tungsten carbide burrs
• Sloyd or carving knife
• File and rasp
• Finishing sander

DIRECTIONS:
1. Measure and cut a series of chunks from 2″ scrap pine. The chunks of wood should vary in size, as the mushrooms have to vary in size and shape. Make some mushrooms tall, and others small; some fat, and some thin. Refer to Illus. 226 and 227 for assistance.
2. Using either a grinder and burr or a knife and

Illus. 226. Mushrooms on a log.

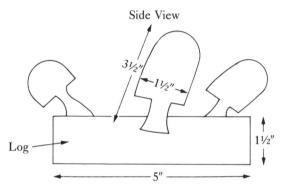

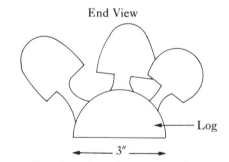

Illus. 227. Drawing of mushrooms on a log.

rasp, shape the mushrooms and their stems. Pine is easy to work with, but does splinter easily. Remember, you are making approximations of a mushroom, not an exact representation. The finishing sander with coarse-grit abrasive paper can also be used to shape the mushrooms.
3. Measure, cut, and slice a piece of log. Re-

148

move any loose bark, but, if possible, leave any bark that is still attached in place.

4. Drive wire brads, partially, into the bottom of the stems of each mushroom. Leave at least ⅜" of the brad sticking out. Using a file, sharpen the heads of the wire brads.

5. Decide where you want to place the mushrooms on the log. Force the sharpened wire brad and the mushroom in place. Repeat the process until all the mushrooms have been secured to the log.

6. Apply several coats of clear lacquer to the mushrooms and the log slice. Add lacquer to the bark, too.

Illus. 228. Wooden bowl.

93: *Wooden Bowl* (Illus. 228

and 229)

This turned black walnut bowl can be used as a decorative desktop or mantel piece, or even as a pencil holder. An oil or lacquer finish brings out the character of the black walnut. However, wood other than black walnut can be used for the project. Note how the sapwood has been exploited on the project bowl.

MATERIAL:
- 3¾" (15/4's) thick black walnut
- Oil or lacquer

TOOLS:
- Wood lathe and turning tools
- Chuck
- Band saw
- School compass
- Finishing sander

DIRECTIONS:
1. Using a school compass and band saw, trace and cut a turning block for the project.
2. If you do not have a commercial chuck, use a glue block and a faceplate.
3. Secure the assembly on the lathe and turn it to shape. Use a revolving center in the tailstock,

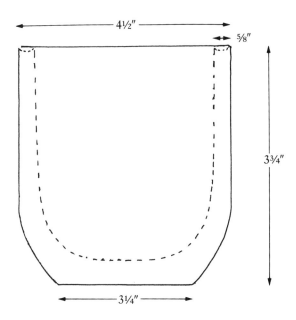

Illus. 229. Drawing of wooden bowl.

and bring it forward against the block while turning. This not only lends stability to the block while it is being turned, but also provides a measure of safety.

A bowl gouge or a 1" roundnose scraper will serve you well as you turn the bowl. The project bowl has a concave edge at the top of the bowl.
4. Remove the turned bowl from the chuck or glue block and clean up the bottom surface with the finishing sander.
5. Finish the bowl with either oil or a clear lacquer.

94: *Shorebird 6* (Illus. 230

and 231)

This bird takes less wood than the previous ones, and is a bit easier to make. Refer to Gift Project 4 to obtain some specific directions in carving or shaping the bird.

MATERIAL:
• 3″ (12/4's) thick basswood

• ¼″ dowel
• ⅛″ dowel
• Chunk of firewood
• Lacquer

TOOLS:
• Band saw
• Electric grinder
• Large tungsten carbide burrs
• Carving or sloyd knife
• Electric drill and ¼″ and ⅛″ bits
• Finishing sander

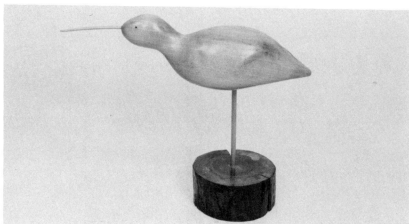

Illus. 230. Shorebird 6.

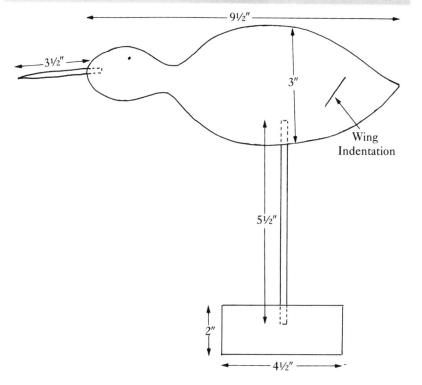

Illus. 231. Drawing of shorebird 6.

DIRECTIONS:

1. Draw an outline of the bird on the surface of the basswood, or make a pattern and trace it. Using a band saw and a ¼″ blade, cut out the carving block. You may want to remove some of the excess wood using the band saw.

2. Refer to Illus. 230 and 231 for design ideas. For assistance in carving and shaping the bird, refer to Gift Project 4.

3. Make a wing indentation on this bird. Note its location in Illus. 230 and 231. Simply remove some wood from this area to convey the impression of a wing.

4. Drill a ⅛″ diameter hole in the bill area of the head. Cut a length of ⅛″ dowel, sharpen the front end, and glue the back end into the drilled hole.

5. Drill a ¼″ hole into the bottom center of the bird. Cut a piece of ¼″ dowel to length to use to support and display the bird.

6. Cut a slice of log to size, drill a ¼″ diameter hole in its center, and place the support dowel, secured to the bird, in the hole.

7. Finish the bird with clear lacquer. Rub it with steel wool (0000) between coats. Apply a coat of paste wax for a final finish.

95: *Heart Desktop Pen-and-Paper-clip Holder* (Illus. 232 and 233)

This desktop pen-and-paper-clip holder is made from black walnut and in the shape of a heart. If you lack a lathe, simply omit the clip holder area. The size of the holder can also be varied, to meet a particular need. And oak or some other hardwood can be used with the black walnut, in order to coordinate woods. As always, design the final project the way you want it to be. The pen set can be obtained from a mail-order supplier or a local craft store.

MATERIAL:
• ¾″ (3/4's) thick hardwood

• Pen set
• Mineral oil or lacquer

TOOLS:
• Sabre or scroll saw
• Wood lathe and turning tools
• Electric drill, and ½″ and ⅛″ bits
• Table-mounted router and roundover bit
• Finishing sander

DIRECTIONS:

1. Make a pattern of a heart to the suggested project dimensions. Trace the pattern on a piece of hardwood and cut it.

2. If you plan to turn a paper-clip area, secure a glue block and faceplate to the bottom center of the heart. Turn the area to the suggested diameter. Be careful not to turn it too deep and go through the bottom of the heart. Remove the glue block and sand the bottom of the heart.

3. Rout the edges using a roundover bit.

4. Prepare the heart for finishing either with an electric sander or by hand. Wipe off the sanding dust.

5. Finish the project with oil or a clear lacquer.

6. Mark the location of the pen set. Depending upon the type of pen, secure it to the heart. Some sets come with an adhesive on the base. On others, holes have to be drilled in and through the bottom surface so that the funnel can be attached with a small bolt. Follow the directions in Gift Project 1 for assistance with this task.

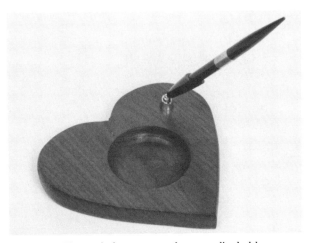

Illus 232. Heart desktop pen-and-paper-clip holder set.

Illus. 233. Drawing of heart desktop pen-and-paper-clip holder set.

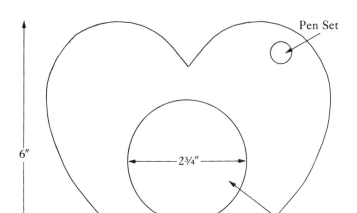

6½"

6"

Pen Set

2¾"

Paper-Clip Area

96: *Candle Holder* (Illus. 234 and 235)

Wood turners will find this a fun project to make, and one that will prove to be a great gift. People love tall, turned candle holders, especially when they're made from black walnut. The bottom of the holders can be covered with felt, to prevent the scratching of the table surface or other surfaces.

MATERIAL:
- 2" (8/4's) thick hard walnut
- 1" (4/4's) thick hard walnut
- ½" dowel
- Felt
- Lacquer or mineral oil

TOOLS:
- Band saw
- Wood lathe and turning tools
- Drill press and ½" and ⅞" bits
- Clamp
- School compass
- Finishing sander

DIRECTIONS:
1. Measure and cut a turning spindle for the holder. Refer to Illus. 235 for assistance.
2. Using a school compass, draw a round pattern on the black walnut. This will be the block for the base. Cut the pattern with a band saw.
3. Locate and mark the center of the holder spindle and the base. Drill a ½" diameter hole in both. The hole should be at least ½" deep.

Illus. 234. Candle holder.

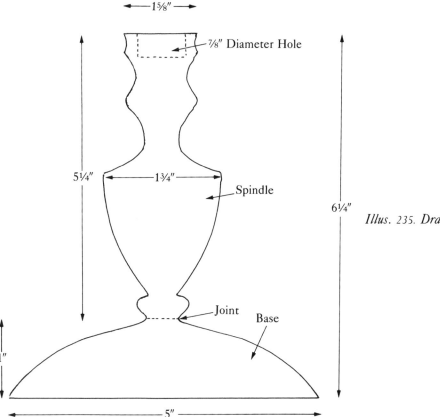

Illus. 235. Drawing of candle holder.

4. Cut a 1″ long piece of ½″ dowel. Spread glue in the drilled holes and tap the dowel into one of them. Spread wood glue on the surfaces of the spindle and the base, insert the other end of the dowel in place, and clamp. Allow the glue to dry. The dowel will give added strength to the holder both when it's being turned and used.

5. Center and secure a faceplate directly to the base. Use short screws. Remember that these screws are in the base when you're turning the holder. Thread the assembly on the lathe. Use a revolving center in the tailstock to support the assembly. The point will also mark the center where the candle hole is to be drilled. Turn as desired.

6. Remove the faceplate. Drill a ⅞″ diameter hole in the top of the spindle to hold a candle. If you are using a candle with a different base diameter, drill a hole of the appropriate diameter. Drill the hole with the appropriate sized bit.

7. Prepare the base and the top for finishing with a sander. If you plan to cover the base with felt,

leave the screw holes from the faceplate unfilled.
8. Finish the holder with either oil or lacquer. Secure a piece of felt or felt dots to the bottom surface.

97: *Necklace Holder* (Illus. 236 and 237)

Made from pine and comprised of small Shaker pegs, this holder is well suited for placement on a dresser. It allows the user to keep necklaces separate and untwisted. Rings can be placed on dowels in the base.

MATERIAL:
- 1″ x 10″ pine
- 2″ x 4″ pine
- ¼″ dowels
- Mini Shaker pegs
- Paint

Illus. 236. Necklace holder.

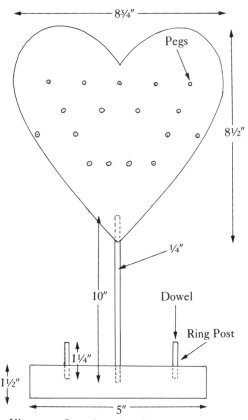

Illus. 237. Drawing of necklace holder.

154

TOOLS:

- Sabre or scroll saw
- Table-mounted router and roundover bit
- Electric drill and ¼" bit
- Finishing sander

DIRECTIONS:

1. To get a perfect heart, make a pattern using Illus. 239 as a guide. Trace and cut the heart.

2. Measure and mark the location of the pegs on the surface of the heart. Place the pegs so that each necklace can hang freely without entanglement with any other necklace. This holder has 14 Shaker pegs. If you use ¼" diameter dowels in place of pegs, there will be more room for the necklaces to hang.

3. Drill ¼" diameter holes to receive the tenons of the mini Shaker pegs.

4. Measure and cut the base from a piece of 2" x 4" stock.

5. Rout the edges of the heart and base with a roundover bit.

6. Measure and mark the location of the support piece and the two ring posts on the base. Drill ¼" diameter holes where marked. The depth of the ring-post holes should be the same. Cut two 1¼" long pieces of ¼" dowel and glue them into the ring-post holes.

7. Drill a ¼" diameter hole at the center, bottom point of the heart. The hole should be at least ½" deep. Cut a 10" long piece of ¼" dowel for a support piece.

8. Prepare the project for painting and paint it. The base can also be decorated.

9. Secure the support dowel in the base and the hole in the bottom of the heart.

98: Corkscrew

(Illus. 238 and 239)

This corkscrew will nicely complement the wine rack project on pages 123 and 124. The handle of this corkscrew is turned from a piece of black walnut. It holds a nickel-plated screw that is available from mail-order suppliers. It can be made from cherry or maple scrap.

MATERIAL:
- 1½″ (6/4's) thick black walnut (scraps)
- Corkscrew
- Lacquer

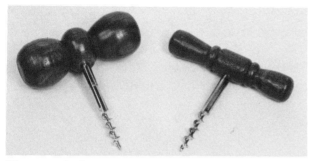

Illus. 238. Corkscrews.

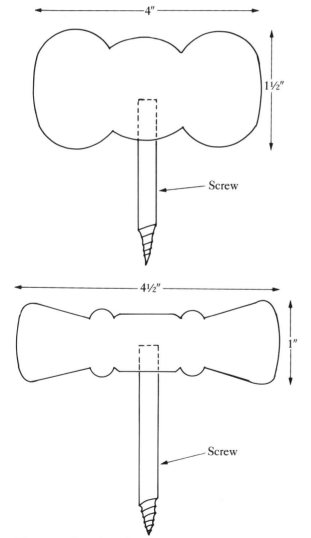

Illus. 239. Drawing of corkscrews.

TOOLS:
- Wood lathe and turning tools
- Chuck
- Band saw
- Electric drill and ¼″ bit
- Pliers

DIRECTIONS:

1. Measure and cut turning spindles to the desired length and thickness. The size of the scraps should determine the size of the handle.
2. If you don't have a commercial chuck, turn the spindles between a drive and revolving center.
3. Drill a ¼″ diameter hole in the center of the handle to accommodate the threaded portion of the corkscrew.
4. Squirt some wood glue in the hole and thread in the corkscrew. Pliers will help in twisting the corkscrew into the hole. Be careful not to scratch the screw's surface with the pliers.
5. Lacquer the handle. When it is dry, test the corkscrew.

99: *Ring-Toss Game*

(Illus. 240 and 241)

This easy-to-make game will prove enjoyable for both youngsters and adults. The rules are simple: At a predetermined distance, try to throw a ring over the dowel. Paint the various game parts with bright colors.

MATERIAL:
- 1″ x 8″ pine
- 1″ dowels
- ⅝″ hemp rope
- Wood screws
- Wood and white glue
- Paint

TOOLS:
- Sabre saw
- Drill press, vise, and ⅝″ bit
- Table-mounted router and roundover bit
- Finishing sander

Illus. 240. Ring-toss game.

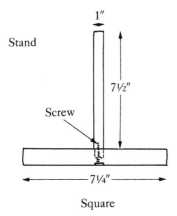

Illus. 241. Drawing of ring-toss game.

DIRECTIONS:

1. Measure and cut two 7¼″ square bases.

2. Rout the edges of the bases with a roundover bit.

3. Measure and cut two 7½″ long, 1″ diameter dowels.

4. Locate and mark the center of the bases on the bottom surfaces. Thread a wood screw through the base at the marked center, with its point protruding through the top surface. Spread wood glue on one end of a dowel, and center and tap it on the screw point. Finish screwing the dowel to the surface of the base. Repeat the process with the second base and dowel.

5. Cut four 1½″ long pieces of a 1″ diameter dowel. Drill a ⅝″ diameter hole though each dowel piece. You may have to use a drill press vise to hold the dowels while drilling. Make sure that the holes are centered in the dowels.

6. Measure and cut four 15″ long pieces of ⅝″ diameter hemp rope. Hemp rope will probably be available at a local hardware store. It makes the best rings for the game.

7. Using a sander, slightly round the outside edge of each dowel piece. Also, round over the top edge of each dowel post.

8. Spread white glue on the ends of the rope and inside the dowel pieces. Insert the ends of the rope into the dowel. Repeat the process for all the rings. Allow the glue to dry.

9. Paint the ring dowels two different colors so that the players can identify their rings.

10. Paint the dowel posts yellow and their tops red. This gives them a colorful look and also makes them easier to see. The base can also be decorated.

100: *Teddy Bear Shelf*

(Illus. 242 and 243)

Any child will thoroughly enjoy this teddy bear shelf. In addition to being able to place items on the shelf, the child can also hang coats, hats, or other items of clothing on the Shaker pegs extending from the support piece. While the project is useful at the size presented, it can be made larger. It's very easy to simply extend its length without changing the other dimensions. This gift has a lot of surface on which to paint and decorate.

MATERIAL:
- 1″ x 8″ pine
- 1″ x 4″ pine
- Shaker pegs
- Finishing nails and wood glue

TOOLS:
- Sabre saw
- Scroll saw
- Band saw
- Table-mounted router and roundover bit
- Electric drill and ½″ bit
- Countersink drill
- Finishing sander

DIRECTIONS:
1. Make a pattern of the bear using construction paper. Refer to Illus. 243 for dimensions. Trace and cut the bear. Remember, two bears are needed for this project.

2. Measure and cut the shelf and the support piece.

3. Measure and mark the location of the Shaker pegs on the support piece. Drill ½″ diameter holes where marked to hold the peg tenons.

4. Drill hanging holes through the support piece using the countersink.

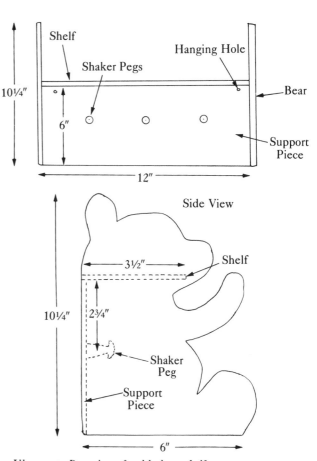

Illus. 243. Drawing of teddy bear shelf.

Illus. 242. Teddy bear shelf.

5. Rout the edges of the various parts. Do not rout edges that will connect to other parts. For example, do not rout the ends of the shelf piece because they will be attached to the sides of the bears.

6. Prepare all surfaces and edges for painting using the finishing sander. Wipe off the dust.

7. Using glue and finishing nails, attach the shelf piece to the top edge of the support piece.

8. Attach a bear to each end of the shelf and support piece with wood glue and finishing nails. Using a nail set, drive all nail heads under the surface of the wood.

9. Spread glue on the Shaker peg tenons and tap them into the holes in the support piece.

10. Paint and decorate the project. Eyes and a mouth can be added to each bear. Don't forget the ears and the nose.

101: Pig Cutting Board

(Illus. 244 and 245)

This is the type of gift that you should consider making in quantity. They don't take a lot of wood and they're practical. An added feature is a tag that is tied to the tail. You can write a message on the tag or emblazon your logo. Make the boards from hard rock maple, and finish them with mineral oil.

MATERIAL:
- ¾″ (3/4's) thick hard maple
- ³⁄₁₆″ thick hard maple
- String
- Mineral oil

TOOLS:
- Sabre, scroll, or band saw
- Table-mounted router and roundover bit
- Electric drill and ⅛″ and ⅜″ bits
- Finishing sander

DIRECTIONS:
1. Make a pattern of both pigs using construction paper. Refer to Illus. 244 and 245 for dimensions and design ideas.
2. Trace the larger pattern on ¾″ thick hard maple and cut it.
3. Rout the edges of the pig with a roundover bit.
4. Drill a ⅜″ diameter hole in the tail area.
5. Trace the smaller pig on ³⁄₁₆″ thick stock and cut it. Drill a ⅛″ diameter hole in the tail area.
6. Using an electric sander, prepare the surfaces and edges for finishing.
7. Finish the cutting board with mineral oil. Use a piece of string to connect the two pigs.

Illus. 244. Pig cutting board.

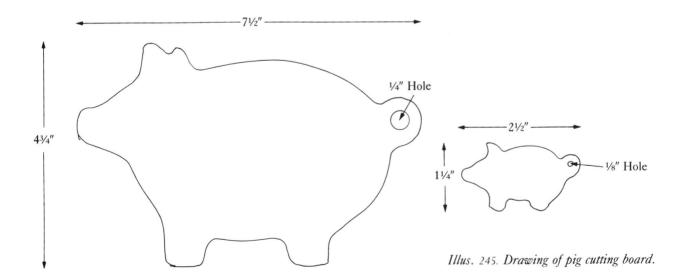

Illus. 245. Drawing of pig cutting board.

7½″

4¾″

¼″ Hole

2½″

1¼″

⅛″ Hole

Acknowledgments

I wish to acknowledge and thank the following companies for providing photographs and granting permission to use them: Stanley Tools, Division of The Stanley Works, New Britain, Ct.; Delta International Machinery Corp., Pittsburgh, Pa.; Dremel, Racine, Wi.; Makita U.S.A., Inc., Mt. Prospect, Il.; Black & Decker, Hunt Valley, Md.; Porter-Cable Professional Power Tools, Jackson, Tn.; Woodworks, Fort Worth, Tx.

Acknowledgments and thanks are also extended to the following individuals for providing both ideas and projects: Wendell Meyer, Meyer's Woodcraft, Belleville, Il.; P.J. O'Neill, Alton, Il.; Leanne DeLaurenti, Pocahontas, Il.

A very special thanks to Andy Matoesian, Granite City, Il., and Peter J. Jacobson, Namibia, SWA, for their assistance.

Metric Equivalents

INCHES TO MILLIMETRES AND CENTIMETRES

MM—millimetres   CM—centimetres

Inches	MM	CM	Inches	CM	Inches	CM
⅛	3	0.3	9	22.9	30	76.2
¼	6	0.6	10	25.4	31	78.7
⅜	10	1.0	11	27.9	32	81.3
½	13	1.3	12	30.5	33	83.8
⅝	16	1.6	13	33.0	34	86.4
¾	19	1.9	14	35.6	35	88.9
⅞	22	2.2	15	38.1	36	91.4
1	25	2.5	16	40.6	37	94.0
1¼	32	3.2	17	43.2	38	96.5
1½	38	3.8	18	45.7	39	99.1
1¾	44	4.4	19	48.3	40	101.6
2	51	5.1	20	50.8	41	104.1
2½	64	6.4	21	53.3	42	106.7
2	76	7.6	22	55.9	43	109.2
3½	89	8.9	23	58.4	44	111.8
4	102	10.2	24	61.0	45	114.3
4½	114	11.4	25	63.5	46	116.8
5	127	12.7	26	66.0	47	119.4
6	152	15.2	27	68.6	48	121.9
7	178	17.8	28	71.1	49	124.5
8	203	20.3	29	73.7	50	127.0

Index